PASTORAL THEOLOGY

AND

SCIENCE

SIX LECTURES

ON

PASTORAL THEOLOGY

WITH AN APPENDIX

ON

THE INFLUENCE OF SCIENTIFIC TRAINING
ON THE RECEPTION OF RELIGIOUS TRUTH

BY

THE VEN. JAMES M. WILSON, D.D.,

VICAR OF ROCHDALE, AND ARCHDEACON OF MANCHESTER;
LECTURER ON PASTORAL THEOLOGY IN THE UNIVERSITY OF CAMBRIDGE IN 1903

London

MACMILLAN AND CO., LIMITED

NEW YORK: THE MACMILLAN COMPANY

1903

PREFACE

THE following Lectures were written for, and delivered to, young University laymen who were contemplating Holy Orders. The Appendix is a dissertation, not a lecture, on a different but kindred subject on which I had been requested to write. The Lectures and Appendix have been written piecemeal, amid the stress of varied and constant work, and this must be the apology for their style.

The selection of subjects was partly made for me, as will be seen by reference to the footnote on p. 4. But the treatment of them has been mainly determined by conversation and correspondence for years past with young laymen and clergy. I know how difficult it is, perhaps impossible, for any one to enter into the thoughts and needs of men of active minds forty years younger than himself. This, however, is what I have tried to do; and they alone can be judges how far I may have succeeded in helping them to see that the ministry of the Church of England is possible to men who feel the call to pastoral work, but dare not sacrifice intellectual honesty and activity, and freedom to "follow the gleam."

The Lectures do not profess to do more than deal with "attitudes of mind." They touch principles: they do not enter into details. But I am well aware that on details also guidance to ordinands is much desired and needed, and such guidance should be extremely clear and plain. How are they to view and to teach Bible stories, such as the Creation, the Fall, and the Flood, or the giving of the Law, and in general the miraculous narratives of the Old Testament? What may they say, and when, and how? And New Testament problems, and the interpretation of the relation of the language to the substance of the Creeds, call for the most truthful and spiritual teaching. Some of these questions, and others going deep into philosophy, have been brought to me in private. No lectures to young clergy and ordinands would be more useful than conversations on such difficulties. It is difficult to believe that such difficulties were entirely unfelt at any epoch, by any individual, however simple : the "assent" of a thoughtful conscience must always, one would think, have been subject to some qualification. But now the Ethics of assent and of conformity have for obvious reasons become more difficult; and it is wiser to face these difficulties and go on, than to shut our eyes, or even go back.

In these Lectures and Appendix there is nothing, I believe, which is at all startling or novel : the thoughts and principles are either familiar to most of us, or such as all may accept.

But in the application of these principles there is work for many years to come, work which will tax the heads and the hearts of the generation to whom I speak. " I write unto you, young men, because ye are strong, and the Word of God abideth in you."

JAMES M. WILSON.

ROCHDALE VICARAGE,
May 1903.

CONTENTS

CONTENTS

SECTION I

SECTION II

SECTION III

SECTION IV

LECTURE I

ABSTRACT

THE limitation implied in the word " pastoral."

The method of study of theology, compared with that of the study of the natural sciences. Theology rests on human experience and thoughts. Hence "pastoral theology" suggests the theology of pastoral experience, the scientific study of God's revelation of Himself in man. This involves the study of revelation in the past, and the tests of its truth. There is a progress in revelation, and therefore in theology. Relation of experience to revelation, and to certain doctrines of revelation in particular.

The fundamental assumption in the word "theology." The substitution of moral idealism for belief in a living God inconsistent with theology. Its essential weakness. The danger of reaction at the present day from materialistic dogmatism into moral idealism.

The distinctive marks of the pastoral spirit—the belief that every one "has a soul to save"; that Christian faith is the permanent factor in human progress; a deep sense of sin and struggle; a desire to set forth Christian truth; a sincere respect for others; a sense of the need of self-consecration.

I

THE MEANING OF "PASTORAL THEOLOGY," AND THE ESSENTIAL QUALIFICATIONS OF THE PASTOR.

THIS course of lectures does not follow quite the ordinary lines. It is an attempt, so far as is compatible with the conditions of this lecture-ship and with my own limitations, to offer some help to those who are contemplating Holy Orders, by emphasising alike the unalterable essentials for the work of the ministry, and the large growth and latitude in thought and opinion and action that such work permits and invites; to place theology before you, not as a study which you can master now up to a certain point in a text-book, but as a continued course of combined observation and research. It is an attempt to outline some of the opportunities for raising the ideals of the nation, for which a post in the ministry of our Church offers advantages, not attainable by most of us in any other way; to suggest the far-reaching national importance of a true and noble Christian theology; to fortify and enrich faith by showing how once more Christianity is absorbing truth from all sides, and in particular from the immense development of scientific methods of observation and reasoning, as well as from the results of historical criticism of our documents and of our institutions. Finally, it is an attempt to give, as far as time will permit, some practical suggestions as to the life, teaching, aims, and activities of those who thus devote themselves to the interests of the pastoral ministry of the Church. I aim, it will be seen, rather at showing our increased power of attack than at strengthening our lines of defence.

It is an immense programme, far beyond my powers to deal with as I could wish ; but it is for this that the Electoral Board[1] has sum-

[1] " It has been the deliberate policy of the Board to treat the field of ' Pastoral Theology ' in the widest possible way, securing lectures upon very various portions of it. This time it was not so much the wish of the Board to provide lectures on ordinary parochial work.

moned me, and I cannot shirk the task. It
would be far easier to deal either with the
important questions of parochial organisation
and method and order, or with suggestions for
the discipline of personal life and for study ; but
I think it my duty to attempt to bring these
large, vital, central questions, which lie at the
root of our ministry, into the teaching offered
to ordinands from the University, however
inadequately I may do it, in hope that others
more qualified for such work may continue and
supplement, and if need be correct, my teaching.
Lectures of this kind are wanted, to prevent
the undue and mistaken limitation of candidates
for Holy Orders. But some few preliminary
remarks are necessary.

Pastoral Theology.—What is meant and
implied by the adjective "pastoral" in this

That branch of pastoral theology has been amply treated of late. The
series was to give our intending clergymen some guidance with regard
to the kind of difficulties of belief that they would be likely to meet
with in the course of an ordinary ministry, and the wisest mode of
dealing with them. . . . The Board did not indeed wish to tie
you down to that particular line of instruction, but to leave you quite
free to choose your own subjects. Its hope, however, was in the
direction I have tried to indicate." (Letter to Archdeacon Wilson
from Professor Mason, 18th February 1902.)

connection? It is a limitation of some kind.
These are not to be lectures on theology in
general. But what exactly is the limitation?
Is it to the theology that finds its source and
sanction in pastoral work? Or to the theology
that is specially needed for pastoral work? Or
are these really identical? And are we quite
clear what we mean by the substantive
"theology"? Let us begin by trying to think
out the meaning of these two words. Pastoral
theology is not the same thing as pastoral *care*
or pastoral *work*.

If I were announced to give a course of
lectures on geology (to take that as a specimen
of the natural sciences), you would all know
perfectly well from what basis I should start.
I should start with the visible, tangible materials
of which the earth is composed, their arrangement and distribution, and the actions now
at work modifying these arrangements. And
having laid before you a sufficiently broad
basis of familiar facts, partly tested by our own
eyes and hands in specimens, partly exhibited
by photographs and maps and drawings, partly
confirmed by others whose observations we

trust, I should proceed to build up a connected provisional theory of the structure of
the earth, of its gradual formation and history ;
not forgetting, indeed, to point out our complete
ignorance of origins, the vast gaps in our
knowledge, and the inequality of evidence for
different parts of the theory ; and to indicate
the points still needing investigation, and to
draw a warning from the failure of some early
theories ; but showing how, in general, the
theory embraces the facts, so far as they are
known, and the facts verify the theory.   Such
is the method adopted in teaching natural
science.

Now is there anything corresponding to all
this in the study of theology ?   Of course it
is not a physical science, and I cannot illustrate
it by specimens and photographs, and verify its
results by experiment.   In some respects it
is more analogous to history and philosophy.
But, *mutatis mutandis*, is the method of study
and of teaching the same ?   Is there, in other
words, in theology a basis of verifiable facts on
which verifiable inductions rest ?   And if so,
what is that basis ?

I say at once that there is such a basis of
facts, and that it lies in human hearts and
human experience, and in the laws of human
thought; and that since the work of the pastor
should bring him constantly into living,
sympathetic touch with these human hearts,
he has the means of ceaselessly testing,
purifying, enlarging, correcting his theology.
His theology may at last, therefore, be called
pastoral, because it is tested, enlarged, purified,
verified by his pastoral experience.

This then is one meaning of the limiting adjective " pastoral," and helps us to distinguish
the subject of these lectures from historic, from
systematic or dogmatic, and from metaphysical
theology.   These may be the work of a student
in his library; but the student of pastoral
theology must be himself a pastor in some
degree, a pastor in spirit.   In truth he must
be a man that is in touch and sympathy with
human life, drawing from man, as from an ex-
haustless fountain of experience, fresh evidence,
fresh illustrations, of his teaching about God.
It is on this ground that theology must be
regarded as a science.   In natural science, as

Lord Bacon said, "*omnia a rebus ipsis petenda sunt*"; and so the pastor draws his theory slowly, hesitatingly, modestly, *a rebus ipsis*. They may often perplex him; but these facts of human nature, intractable as they are, form the material of his science.   We all have to learn to respect facts—"to see things as they are," as nearly as we can.   Theological beliefs are not the invention of priests or philosophers, which could be altered by the will of man; they are not the dicta of an infallible or authoritative Church; they are not inferences from an infallible book; they arise ultimately out of the nature of things; they are rooted in human nature; they are verified by ever-renewed and ever-enriched human experience; they arise out of the one eternal thing, the eternal mystery—life in God and man.   And just as the study of natural philosophy or of natural history assumes a fresh dignity and worth when it is seen to be the study of God's work, of God's self-revelation in the laws of nature and of life, so the study of theology assumes a fresh reality and interest when it is seen to be the scientific study of God's

revelation of Himself in man, and His supreme
and unique revelation of Himself in Christ.

I am emphasising this unfamiliar aspect of
the word "pastoral." The work of the pastor
has the surpassing and truly scientific interest
of bringing men into contact with facts—facts
of the deepest interest, psychological, philosophical, historical. The facts are not easily
defined or isolated; they have to be studied by
the large and loving heart, as well as by the
logical head and the trained philosophic mind
—*pectus facit theologum;* and both heads and
hearts make mistakes if they go far from facts,
or view them through the disturbing and
blinding influences of prepossessions. Such a
study of theology may well be called pastoral.
It is an essential element in the development
of man's knowledge of himself and of God;
and it grows as living bodies grow, by the
perpetual assimilation of new matter from
without, and the perpetual rejection of that
which has done its work.

The pastor will be very modest in his
attitude towards truth; but he should always
be conscious that he may contribute something

from his own experience to advance or correct the sum total of human experience which finds its expression in theology. This is the privilege and inspiration of all scientific study. Facts are what they are: we cannot alter them. Our explanations may change, must change: the facts remain. We master nature, and find her unsuspected powers, by studying and obeying her. Is it not equally true to say that in the same way we shall find out and justify God's will for man?

No one will, I hope, understand me to say that every one has to construct his own theology afresh for himself. Behind our Christian theology lies an immense mass of fact and of the experiences of others. But nevertheless the result is not final; the record of human experience is not closed. Life is an ever-flowing, widening stream. In geology the accepted theory is of immense value; coal-miners and railway contractors, and all sorts of practical men, use the accumulated knowledge acquired by the past, which is incorporated into the theory, and made common property; they use it as a framework, but they also ceaselessly

modify and extend and correct it. It is
difficult to say of the theoretic geologist and
the practical man which owes the larger debt
to the other.

It is precisely so in the case of theology.
The test of the value of doctrine is its making
for righteousness—its lifting men nearer to
God—and this test is applied in the life of a
nation in the work of the religious teacher.
The pastor corresponds to the practical man.
Unconsciously the pastorate drops, first tacitly,
then explicitly, such theoretic teaching as does
not make for truth and righteousness, and then
after a time that teaching drops out of the
theoretic science also.   How, for example, has
the doctrine of everlasting punishment, in the
physical sense in which it used to be taught,
dropped out?   Not only because it is
seen to be inconsistent with the whole
thought of God as revealed in and by Christ ;
but also because it has been shown by experience not now to make for righteousness ;
not to deter from sin, but to make for horror,
and disbelief, and aversion from God.   And
then the theologian finds that after all the

doctrine was only accommodated to the time, that αἰώνιος may have another meaning; and the material hell drops out of dogmatic, as out of pastoral, theology. Progress in systematic theology comes by the slow progress of which this is an instance, and every faithful and truth-loving pastor contributes to this progress.

The pastor therefore must always be a learner, and he will be specially helped by the wisest and holiest minds to interpret his own experience, and to plant his own feet firm on that sure and eternal rock, the Word of God in the human soul. He must verily become as a little child.

If a young pastor begins his work humbly, knowing that he is entering on the infinite field of human relationship to God, with some clue indeed, some outline map of the region, in the faith and experience of all who have gone before, but not yet the intimate knowledge that comes with personal experience;—if he has an intense love of truth and a scientific habit of mind that tests and verifies all that presents itself to him as true;—he will find to his joy that the old message which he will find

everywhere, in Psalm and in Prophet as well
as in the Gospels, still reaches the heart—

The Lord does know the way of the righteous,
And the way of the wicked perishes.

And this truth, reached in this way, carries a
cogency and conviction that is won in no other
way.

Now I can conceive a reverent and thoughtful mind among you saying, "If theology is,
as you seem to say, based on human experience, what is revelation? I thought we got
our theology, our knowledge of God, by
revelation." But, I ask, are the two statements incompatible? Does revelation come
to the world otherwise than through human
experience? Is it written in the clouds of
heaven? Is not all the revelation in the Old
Testament given us in the lives and words of
men? Is not the revelation given us by our
Lord Jesus Christ given to us in His human
life, and expressed in terms of verifiable human
experience? And do we not believe that at
this day the Holy Spirit is guiding and teaching us in terms of human experience? There

is, of course, a Deism which makes its God—if
there is a God in Deism—infinitely remote from
men. With that Deism I have no concern.
But if we believe in God's Fatherhood at all,
we believe that there is in us something of the
divine Life, and that what is best in us reveals
its origin. That belief in the divine rests on
the bed - rock of experience. The thoughts
and aspirations of the best men, the experience
of the saints living and dead, are in themselves
a revelation. We are surrounded by revelation ; it is not limited to the past. There is a
revelation in us, as well as to us. The two
things, therefore, that we speak of, and may
even for a moment contrast, the experience of
man and the revelation from God, are essentially one thing ; the supernatural is always
passing into the natural ; there is one path of
communication between God and man. We
look up the path or we look down it, but the
path is the same. And all the past experience
of the world, all its religious treasures, and,
most of all, the unsurpassable treasure of the
revelation in Christ, thus becomes a part of
our own experience, part of the intercommunion

between man and God. This is what is meant
by saying that theology rests on experience;
it is as true of dogmatic as it is of moral
theology, of the sanctions alike of faith and of
conduct.

And it may be worth while to indicate here
how the experience of a pastor almost unconsciously confirms those great truths which
we pre-eminently regard as revealed. The
pastor, *quâ* pastor, has light to throw on the
doctrine of the Incarnation. From the point
of view of the text-books of theology, the
evidence for the Incarnation is mainly historical;
and of course this historical evidence to a fact
in history can never be replaced or dispensed
with, though it can never amount to demonstration. But if his eyes and heart are open,
and his mind humble, the pastor is always
coming across such striking proofs of un-
noticed goodness, such loving and unconsciously beautiful self-sacrifice, perhaps in
quite unexpected places, that he is driven to
acknowledge the incarnation of the divine in
the human life of to-day; and every imperfect
and fragmentary presentation of it is to him an

evidence of the perfection somewhere, some-when. Every sparkle from the rippling sea is a proof of the sun. He is able to see perfect in Jesus Christ the complete manifestation of God, so far as God can be represented in finite humanity, just because he has seen it with reverence, in its imperfect manifestation, in so many humble living men and women. Some of us can but dimly see the divine in the inconspicuous life of labour; we are like the brethren of our Lord, unable to see any-thing divine in the Carpenter of Nazareth, while He was working in His home for daily bread.

There is another remark that will be made by a different class of hearers. "The very word theology," it may be said, "implies that God is a real object of knowledge, and that some knowledge of Him is attainable and attained by man. Are you not going to say something on this great implication?" And the answer is that I am not going to do so. We may set out on the path to find out God by various paths suited to our own temperaments: by the study of apparent design and power in

nature, leading to the thought of an Intellectual Designer and Creator; or we may set
out from the laws of our understanding, which
seem to compel us to assume that nature is
governed by final causes, and that a Being
and Mind, with purpose and will akin to our
own, is the Cause of the Universe; or we
may set out from the moral law within us,
and our consciousness of freedom, which
makes to many men the existence of God
an ethical necessity of thought. With these
and other paths to theology, suggested by
the contemplation of nature, by the laws of
thought, by psychology, by ethics, and by
philosophy generally, we have nothing now
to do, except thus briefly to point to them as
the ways by which, according to men's different
temperaments and environments, some assurance is obtainable by them that the object of
theology is real, and that some knowledge of
God is really within the reach of man.

But I do not deal with this philosophical
question from lack of qualification. Moreover,
one must begin somewhere, and I begin by
assuming the reality of this knowledge. There

is no pastoral theology, and no theology at all, if this belief in the reality of a personal God is an illusion. I think it necessary to say this at the outset in the plainest possible way. And I will explain why.

There is a very strong tendency at present on the part of a religious school of thought to abandon the conclusions both indicated by these converging but difficult lines of thought, and rooted in popular conviction, and to rest their religious teaching on the basis not of the Being of God, but on that of the ethical experience of man alone. This tendency is the natural reaction from excessive dogmatism, and from speaking about God with familiarity and assurance, and with a bold and free anthropomorphism. Men may feel that morality and religion are secure without such theology as that. So they exclaim, " Let theology go—this is an age of inductive science ; we have a secure basis of facts in human nature alone. Ethics and psychology and experience are enough by themselves as guides to conduct. It is not necessary to construct a theology out of them. Religion will survive," they even say, "if men lost belief in God.

Moral idealism will survive with a few, and they must inspire the many."

Whether you are familiar with this way of expressing a tendency of modern thought I do not know. But I am quite sure that some men are largely, even if unconsciously, under the influence of a tendency to substitute this moral idealism for the conscious service of a personal God. This is not a point on which to dilate now. I only call your attention to the fact that in the very title, " Pastoral Theology," we assume the objective reality of God, *quem nosse vivere, cui servire regnare est*. And I wish to insist on my conviction that it is not possible to cut off our belief in a living and present God, and our conscious relation of service to Him, and yet permanently retain, transmit, and strengthen in their growth a moral ideal and the pieties and beauties of human character. The belief in the living God is their root. Cut them off from it, and they will languish and die. " He that cometh to God must believe that he is " (Hebrews xi. 6). There may be truly pastoral work, there are beautiful, almost ideal lives, and a loveliness

of personal goodness, without any formulated
theology, without the conviction of a Divine
Personality. This springs from an ideal of
perfection inborn in heart and mind, which
does not carry with it, of necessity, any sug-
gestion that the ideal exists in God, or has
been manifested in Jesus Christ, or is due in
us to the presence of a Holy Spirit. Not one
word would I say to discourage the efforts of
any such moral idealist who is possessed by
these holy aspirations, even if such a one has
not yet found in intellectual conviction their
goal and realisation. There is a work for such
a man in the world; and the conviction has
come to many as a result of such work. The
apostles followed Christ, and loved Him, and
lived His life, and preached Him, and then
they found out who He was, and received the
Holy Spirit. It is as true as ever it was that
"he that desires to do God's will shall know of
the doctrine." Their desire led to their
knowledge, and then they became the preachers
of Christ.

This moral idealism, noble and lovely as it
is, is not yet theology; least of all is it pastoral

theology : it is the origin of theology, the
purest origin ; it is the aspiration after God, and
assuredly it will find God.   But it is not yet
the theology that the pastor will want.   While
it remains moral idealism it lacks just the
elements of inspiration, of intenseness, of
stability, of communicability, of power over
sin.   Such idealism, when confronted with
widespread moral degradation, with blank indifference and materialism, and when, after
years of labour, it sees no result, then it is
heart-broken.   It lacks the rigidity and the
momentum of a conviction that God is over all
and in all, that He is with us, that the duty
He assigns us is possible.   We may get
stimulus and reinforcement from ideals that
we abstract from humanity, but they are no
substitute for the living God.

Pastoral theology there can be none, and
pastoral work will be insecure, without this
bottom rock of faith in God.   Remember that
in the decaying Roman and Greek worlds
there was a Stoic moral idealism as noble as
man has ever formed ; but Judaism, not
wholly lovely, with its unconquerable faith that

" verily there is a God that judgeth the earth,"
stood strong, when all around tottered, and
attracted many of the finest souls.   And it
was not moral idealism which gave life to the
Christian faith that sprang out of Judaism, but
the intense faith in God revealed in Jesus
Christ as our Father and our Saviour.

I have spoken, you may think, at undue
length on this point.   But I desire to impress
on you that your generation will be called on to
check rather than to reinforce this reaction in
the intellectual world of which I spoke—the
reaction from an excessive dogmatism, un-
relieved by a perspective of great and small,
into a moral idealism with no formulated faith
at all.

The truth is in neither extreme.   The
pastor will find that the strength and grip of
religion on men lies neither in the curious
piling up of authoritative dogma and symbolical rite, nor in the attempted avoidance of
all dogma, and the making religion a mere
emotional or rational statement of ideal
morality, an abstraction of our own ; but in
a strong, reasonable, and reasoned faith in

God our Father as an object of knowledge, and reverence, and service, and love, whose kingdom on earth is the one thing worth working for. We may question the extent of our knowledge of God, question the extent and method of His self-revelation, but it is on his ultimate faith in God and His government of the world that the pastor's strength depends.

This being made clear, I can go on to speak of other convictions of the Christian pastor. One is ever present with him, the distinctive mark of the pastoral spirit—the conviction that "every one has," as it is said, "a soul to be saved." This means that in every child of man is the germ and seed of a divine and heavenly life, destined to struggle for its existence and perfection, and that it is our privilege to study and labour to help that germ to grow. The philosophers express it by insisting that all men have worth—that each man is an end in himself. To state this is to carry conviction of its truth; but to keep it in mind, and to give effect to it, and to add to it the belief that each man is an end not only to himself, but to

God, is another matter. It ought to make us review our pastoral methods—what shall we teach, and how? In science there is advance; it is cumulative, nothing is lost. But the art of life, of self-management, of moral law— why is not this more cumulative? How much of the Bible is the sum of experience? It must be taught as experience, and we must add to that experience. As scientific knowledge is acquired by man's own effort, so the moral laws that mould and govern men and nations are learnt by our effort. We must study our methods and principles. Pastoral life affords a magnificent field for such work; but let no one think that the mechanical adoption of some one else's methods, or the association of the soundest principles, will avail much. It is the sincerity of faith in God and of sympathy with man—it is that quality of soul that finds its natural expression in prayer to God and love of man—that makes the true pastor.

Another ever-present conviction of the Christian pastor is that the Christian faith is the great permanent factor in human progress,

and that in working for it, he is working in the
main path of human development, working
with God, in accordance with the eternal laws
of God, and is necessarily on the winning side.
All his knowledge of other religions, and much
else that he knows, will deepen and strengthen
this conviction, and give him persistency. For
the Christian faith is essentially a belief in our
relationship to God as His children, in our
participation of His eternal Life, and in our
actually holding communion with Him. Hence
in this faith we can, as God does, make present
and future one, and, therefore, work for the
future by that slow process which, looked at
from outside by those who are not taking part
in the work, is called evolution, but seen from
God's point of view is His will and His purpose.
We may make that will and purpose ours.

There is another conviction that is so
essential that I cannot pass it over. If the
pastor is to be strenuous in his work, a true
watchman, he must have a profound sense of
sin, both national and personal. I believe
that without this sense of sin his teaching
must be shallow and lack seriousness. We

must not shrink from the painful and humiliating thought that sinfulness affects ourselves through and through, crippling, limiting, damaging, all we say and do. Only thus can we help others to feel their own sin, and the cruel hold sin has on them, and, therefore, to welcome the new life, and the hope and the power to rise out of sin, that Christ has brought. Nothing else will give us real humility, the most distinctive, the most supernatural, of the Christian virtues. It will never come to us except from the sense of sin.

The pastor is also a teacher, and he ought to be a good teacher. He ought to study and realise the value of educational methods. I am not going to speak now about methods of teaching, in the pulpit or elsewhere, and will only make one remark on the special aim of the teaching which belongs to the pastor. What is that aim? It is not to give proofs of doctrines, such as are given in schools of theology. It is not primarily to give knowledge. Bishop Creighton expressed it admirably (Charge, 21st February 1900):

" To train up our people to a sense of their
responsibility as Christians, and to set forth
Christian truth as something which must be
apprehended from within, and must work out
its fruits in a strong and steadfast character."
It is "that they may have life, and have it more
abundantly." That is the great secret. Did
you ever notice the complete absence of con-
straint and compulsion in our Lord's training
of the Twelve? You should read *Pastor
Pastorum*, by the late Master of Trinity Hall,
to help you to see this. And the result was
that the Twelve turned out so individual, such
men, so inspired, men with strength. May we
not say that our Lord treated them all with
great respect? He is the model of teachers.
God gives to each his own personality, deep
below the signs we see ; and that personality
grows by liberty, by liberty and trust. Trust
the divine in each, and it will respond to your
trust. We come back to the need of profound
respect for our people, as we "set forth Christian
truth as something which must be apprehended
from within." If you once master the thought
that each of those whom you are teaching will

carry on the study through life, you will be
more anxious to lay foundations on which it
will be a joy for him to build, than to complete
a little chamber, the narrowness of which may
soon disgust him with all theology.

If you keep this aim steadily before you, you
will not weaken and dull your intellect and
your conscience, and those of your hearers, by
the constant repetition, so familiar, so deadly,
of "The Church directs us," "The Church
teaches," and similar phrases. They may be
true ; but it is thoroughly bad and deadening
teaching from the point of view of spiritual
education. It does not stimulate and strengthen ;
it numbs and lulls the spiritual consciousness.
Aim at "the apprehension from within," and the
expression in action, and give your people the
joy of finding out that they are thus attaining
to the true spirit of the Church.   It makes all
the difference whether you tell your hearers
that something is true because the Church
teaches it, or that the Church teaches it because
it is true, and that they "know of their own
selves" that it is true. So teach that they
shall desire to learn more : let them hear the

waves of the infinite ocean of truth, of that
truth which inspires to duty.

The pastor should be a teacher, to interest,
to awaken, to lift, to inspire. For nearly all his
congregation the Sunday sermon is their one
opportunity in the week to get this inspiration.
The pastor must never forget that in every
soul before him is the divine Life *in esse* or *in
posse*. Behind those irresponsive, immobile
faces, sermon-proof as they seem, from which
nothing could excite a sparkle, is the soul to
be lifted, and being lifted, into a larger air.
Some possess a depth of feeling, unexpressed,
inexpressible, of which you can form no measure.
Infinite variety of temperament; but what a
unity! The same divine soul, the same eternal
yearning, the same way of life and way of
death before each, the same need of loving
guidance to choose the right path. How much
of the Bible, especially of the Psalms, is on the
art of living rightly and wisely; how much we
need that art; how many of us have "forsaken
the fountains of living water to hew out for themselves cisterns, broken cisterns, that can hold
no water." And it is the one opportunity for

teaching the people how to observe our Lord's commands. We have to hand down, to illustrate, to readapt, our Lord's sayings, which are in fact fundamental rules of life. We have to teach that divine revelation of which the Psalmist speaks—the Law of the Lord, that revelation in the human heart which "fulfils the same part in the world of spirits as the sun does in the world of nature"[1] You have to translate into language that fits the mental aptitudes and habits of your people whatever you have to say on God and man and duty.

I have now explained that the word pastoral implies an ever-renewed life, reality, and progress in your theology, as you learn from the spiritual experiences of your people, while that theology itself is founded on the experience and revelation of the past: I have shown that moral idealism, while it may lead to faith in God, is no adequate and final substitute for that faith; the pastor needs an absolute conviction of God: and I have spoken of other fundamental convictions of the pastor, that

[1] *The Psalms, in three Collections*, by E. G. King, D.D. Deighton, Bell and Co. An excellent work.

every one has a soul in which the divine Life
dwells, that Christianity is essential to national
as well as to individual life, and that our failures
are not failures only, but sins. I added a few
words on our opportunities for teaching, and
our special aim at developing individual strength
and character; and now only one word remains
to be said.

There is one more essential, the feeling of
the duty, the necessity of self-consecration.
On this subject one must needs speak, if one
speaks at all, with deep humility. Of all the
elements that go to make the pastor, this is the
most essential. He can do without much learning, indeed without any other obvious qualification; but not without this feeling of the
necessity of personal holiness, and life in Christ,
to fit him to be the guide and the comfort of
others. " For their sakes I sanctify myself,"
said the Master; and how much more must
His disciples !

Perhaps some of you may regard the life of
self-consecration as that of a recluse, of an
unpractical person. It is not so, as a matter
of fact, among the clergy. It is your practical,

busy, undevout man who does not get the real things done, and makes much noise over the not doing of them; and I mean by the real things, the building up of Christ-like lives: and it is your man of prayer and holiness in whose parish things move quietly on—ὡς ῥεῦμα ἐλαίου ἀψοφητὶ ῥέοντος, as Plato says—and a spirit of holiness is ever present. Is it Mary or Martha that does the work of the parish? Think of Westcott: no one could have called him a man of affairs; and what bishop of our day so influenced affairs? "Influence is the power that distils from a life that is lived in communion with God."[1]

[1] *The Personal Life of the Clergy*, by Canon A. W. Robinson. Longmans.

D

LECTURE II

ABSTRACT

SOCIAL QUESTIONS

INFLUENCE of religious ideals on national welfare. Hence a wide field for usefulness open to the pastor.

The terribly unfavourable conditions of life. What clergy can do indirectly affecting these. The necessity and the hopefulness of work in social matters.

Difficulty of interesting the well-to-do classes. A chief cause is the lack of a strong and simple and true popular theology.

A new ideal needed for industrial and commercial and social life. This must come from theology.

Wherein the popular theology is defective.

The simpler theology of early Christianity.

What its effects may again be.

This is the pastoral theology to which the Church is called.

II

PASTORAL THEOLOGY IN ITS BEARING ON NATIONAL PROGRESS AND WELFARE

In my first lecture I spoke of the nature of pastoral theology and of the pastor's qualifications, mainly with reference to the bearing of our work on individual souls. To-day I wish to speak of its bearing on national welfare.

Some of you, I doubt not, are fired with an ambition and resolve to leave our country as a whole a little better for your having lived. Now I believe that there is no path open to so many, and so full of opportunities for doing this, as the life of a man in Holy Orders. This may seem a daring assertion. It will seem less so when you recall the well-known passage from the opening paragraph of our greatest modern work on Economics, by Professor Marshall.

" Man's character," he says, " has been moulded
by his everyday work, and by the material
resources which he thereby procures, more than
by any other influence, unless it be that of his
religious ideals; in fact, the two great forming
agencies of the world's history have been the
religious and the economic."   Now if there is
any position in the world which gives one a
chance of lifting the " religious ideals," and
thus of strengthening one of " the two great
forming agencies of the world's history," it is
that of the pastoral ministry.   True that one
may do this work in any calling.   But in other
callings we may leave it undone without having
entirely missed our mark.   Not so if our
calling is to the ministry of the Church.

At first, as I have said, our thoughts of the
ministry gather round ideals for individuals.
We will endeavour to awaken and stimulate in
men the sense that they are the children of
God; to teach them the joy of using all their
faculties of body, soul, and spirit; the self-
respect and dignity and the kindliness to others
that mark true manhood; and we will look
forward hopefully to the uplifting of the soul

to God, the loyalty to our Lord, and the sense of the presence of the Holy Spirit. In school, in church, and in the daily influence of life, our aim must be to make " the Gospel of Jesus Christ the Son of God "—the fact of God's loving Fatherhood—a real power in every one's life.

I need not say that this is an essential part of pastoral work. We have primarily to deal with the awakening of men's souls. No social work is more fertile and more lasting than this.

But we soon find the terrible limitations placed on our dealing with individuals. It is obvious enough that in our physical and social life we are intimately and vitally connected with the past and the present; heredity, and the continuity of tradition and manners and morals, are an immense power; and we learn that our moral and spiritual life is only slightly more individual, slightly more independent of its environment, than is our physical life. It is so intimately bound up with the moral and spiritual ideals of those among whom we live that it can scarcely rise above them ; and these in their turn are alike the causes and the consequences of the physical conditions of life. How unfavourable many of these conditions are among large sections of our people we cannot fail to see. So our thoughts lead us to another view of the pastoral functions of the Church. We come to see that one of the great and indispensable functions of the Church, and therefore of our ministry, should be to inspire men with a thought of God and man which shall be utterly inconsistent with acquiescence in any demoralising conditions of life. We of all men must not give way to the thought that things are in a vicious circle, which one can get hold of nowhere. We clergy can get firm hold of them at one point. Truer thoughts of God and of man—of God as the Father, of man as the child ; of God dwelling in man ; in man as he is now, body and soul—a union which the doctrines of the Resurrection and the Ascension forbid us to regard as a purely temporary alliance—these are the beginning. They were the beginning of the revelation made in Christ ; they fired men then with new hopes, and they have not now lost their power, though men may have lost faith in them. They are the beginning, and to teach them is our work. Then follow ideals for man which necessitate the improvement of the material conditions of his life. " The two great world-forming agencies," remember, "are the religious and the economic." The religious force, the uplifting power of a religious ideal, based on a true and inspiring theology, is the only force capable of counteracting the evils that flow from unchecked economic forces. No considerations of individual or national interest and expediency—no necessities for " educating our masters," or of " holding our own in international competition," have a fraction of the power of a religious faith. History is a closed book to us if it does not teach us this.

Take one brief glance at these evils as they are at this day among us, I do not say unchecked, but quite insufficiently checked. To realise the present conditions of life among large classes in our cities is not easy for any of us. It requires study, it requires observation, and it requires above all a very tender human sympathy. I can only tell you briefly that the

conditions of industry are such that there is
a large margin of men in every town so
irregularly employed, as to become demoralised
and ultimately unemployable ; that the slum-
life of our cities, and the conditions of much
labour, are training up generation after generation of boys and girls enfeebled in physique, in
intelligence, and in character; so crowded in
their dwellings that decency is impossible ;
so insufficiently fed that they cannot be efficient
workers with body or mind; so fettered in
choice of work that they must take what comes
first or tramp ; so hopeless and joyless in home-
life, that drink and gambling and immoral
pleasures present irresistible attractions. These
pleasures are the only relief. " Men must have
a maintenance," says Aristotle, " before they
can practise virtue." You must realise that
elementary education is doing very little as yet
to remedy this physical and social degradation
of the lowest class, and of classes just above
the lowest, or even to prevent the growth of an
unemployable class. It has prevented matters
from becoming much worse, but that is all.
By itself it has no inspiring power. It is not

necessarily itself inspired with love, which alone can inspire and regenerate others. You must realise the immense power of an organised liquor traffic, commanding boundless capital, enlisting the support of some decent people who are tempted to take shares, debasing here and there the conscience of magistrates, police, and the general public, as well as spreading universally the temptation to drink, and all the miserable demoralisation that follows drink. You must realise that a very large proportion of the labouring class, especially in our large cities, has no relation whatever to public worship in church or chapel, nor even to any Sunday school; that many districts of our great towns are crowded with people whose whole energies, enfeebled as they are, are taken up with living at all. The total amount of wealth produced is enormous, and yet Mr. Charles Booth tells us that 30.7 per cent of the population of London live in "poverty"; and Mr. Seebohm Rowntree, after an exhaustive examination of the population of York, finds that 27.84 of the people are in "poverty." Think what these numbers imply. "Poverty," in Mr. Rowntree's technical

use of the word, means insufficiency of food,
clothing, warmth, shelter, fresh air, and cleanli-
ness to maintain physical efficiency. It means
inability to do a good day's work. " Poverty "
means ceaseless insecurity as to the future : it
means the deprivation of all minor enjoyments
and recreations and amenities of life that come
from possessing "a margin." There is no
" margin " for them. Think what such a life
must be ! How, under these circumstances,
can there be the full fruits of the Spirit ? All
life other than a feeble physical flicker, an
acuteness born of struggle, and a patience
born of suffering, is rendered impossible, except
in rare instances of unconquerable mental
vitality. Every candidate for Holy Orders
ought to read at least Seebohm Rowntree's
book.

Every clergyman can do something towards
the solution of social questions ; and we may
be well assured that these questions will occupy
the mind of the nation in the coming decades to
an extent that we do not now realise.

It is outside the scope of these lectures to
go into any detail ; I can only here emphasise

to each of you the words: *Nihil humani a te alienum puta*. As teachers we are not limited to teaching about the things of the mind, or of the next world. Any and all knowledge will be useful. As pastors we are pastors of body and mind. As evangelists it is as much our duty to prepare the ground for the seed, as to sow the seed in the ground. Everything that affects the well-being of our people must be our care. We shall find that life and other calls will of themselves impose enough limitations on us, and prevent us from becoming busy-bodies or amateur sanitary inspectors and reformers; but I wish to make it plain that there is nothing that affects the welfare of our people which we ought not to know about and take active interest in. It may also be possible, but it is not easy, to get to know something of the inner working of such great organisations as Trades Unions, Friendly Societies, Co-operative Societies, about which most of us are as ignorant as of what goes on in Nigeria. It is impossible to teach the working man till you begin to learn from him; and he has much to teach an ardent learner.

Each one of us also can do something by example. He should set the example of a life ordered by a spiritual principle, and show its value. We know how example is emphasised in our ordination service—that we are to be "wholesome and godly examples and patterns for our people to follow." We have not only to "sanctify our lives," but to "fashion" them after the rule of Christ. So we must constantly think of what this rule requires. It is not easy to decide the limits of simplicity of personal life. But we are bound to show that we do not want wealth or luxuries, except in so far as they make us better members of society. The social questions in which we pastors are absolutely bound to interest ourselves are such as the following:—Problems and facts of poverty; Charity Organisation principles; the Church Army and its labour homes; the Salvation Army and its shelters; the Temperance problem and its gradual solution; the Housing Question. This last is becoming daily more serious, and is vitally affecting the well-being of the nation. An overcrowded house leaves no room for morality or religion.   In many places a Christian Social Union is formed for the joint study among lay and clergy of these matters.   It is not at all needful that we should often make public utterances on these subjects ; but our knowledge of them will show, and greatly increase, both our sympathy and our usefulness, and save us from many mistakes.   The care of the poor and the sick, whether under the poor-law guardians or not ; protection of children ; care of defective children—all are our business. Who is to inspire a society to good citizenship if not the pastor ?   In every town there are openings for fresh progress which we ought to be the first to see, and to suggest to others. Never try to get the credit for these things : so long as they are done, be content.   The blind, or the deaf and dumb, are not looked after in the town ?   Then make it your business first to get the very best advice as to the principles on which a society should work for them.   There is already great experience ; there are excellent workers : find them out.   Then get personal knowledge of the cases ; then pick your men and women who can and will carry on this work, and when it is launched, leave it. So, too, your town may want district nurses, or free baths for school-children, or swimming instruction, or gymnasia, or playing-fields. Follow the same plan. But if there is any drudgery to be done, do it.

Men must judge for themselves in each case how far it is well to connect these organisations with the Church. Sometimes it will provoke jealousy and do harm; but in any case they must get their inspiration from the Christian spirit. And when such organisations are on an avowedly religious basis, they are as great a help to religion as religion is to them. Think of such organisations as the Girls' Friendly Society, and Communicants' Guilds, St. Andrew's Brotherhood, and the Church Lads' Brigade. How they gain by being at once religious and active. It is a great gain to boys' clubs to have voluntary Bible classes connected with them. Mothers' Meetings, the Mothers' Union, Mens' Unions, etc., for the promotion of good family life, are most useful. Men and women will tolerate gentle suggestions for the good of their children, and find that they are

for their own good too.   I have said nothing of
schools—our interest in these is too great and
too obvious.

The pastor also should know what are the
influences that are degrading his people.
There are all sorts of contrivances to induce
women and boys, as well as men, to drink in
public-houses; there are clubs which are little
better than dens of immorality; wine-lodges
are much the same.   There are the low, if not
absolutely indecent, papers circulated among
children.   The pastor must have his eyes open,
and then his heart will be moved, and he will
find the work of his life so interesting that he
will wonder why everybody does not try to
flock into it.   At fifty he will feel like thirty,
and at seventy like forty.   He will wish
that a day had forty-eight hours, and a week
fourteen days; he will wish he was infinitely
better read, cleverer, quicker than he is,
and only regret that he leaves so much un-
touched, and that he will die before he sees
more than a fragment done of what might be
done.

I do not here enter on the question what

E

direct part clergy ought to take in urging
social reforms. All such reforms are closely
bound up with social, economical, and legislative questions, often of a very highly technical
kind. As clergy we have no special knowledge
of these questions which entitles us to speak
with authority, and if we touch these matters
in the pulpit we are felt at once to be taking an
unfair advantage of " Coward's Castle." We
ought, however, to keep before ourselves and
our people the existence of these evils and
their terrible consequences, and constantly
show how by our own personal actions each
man can do something to lessen them. We
must show that we feel, as Plato said, that
" doing injustice is a greater evil than suffering
it." We must make it clear that Christianity
is a life, not a creed only ; and that Christianity
is really on its trial : can it, or can it not,
grapple with the evils of a commercial and industrial age and nation ? I, for one, am sure
that it cannot, unless it inspires far more of
respect for all men as truly our brothers in
Christ than it has yet inspired in our nation.
We clergy cannot accept the present relation of

classes as according with the mind of Christ. We resist selfish individualism, and if we are not prepared to accept socialism as a political and economical programme for reform, it must be because we insist no less than socialists on brotherhood and mutual service as an all-pervading voluntary principle in business transactions as in all domestic relations. And we must not despair of this. What wonderful changes last century—to take only that short period—saw in the tone and aims of our Church. Within your lifetime you may witness—you may assist in bringing about—a still greater revolution. Some day—why not soon?—we shall see in Christ's constant use of His power to relieve the suffering of men, a direct call to use all our wonderful resources of science, and intelligence, and love, in the bettering of our social conditions. Surely an age of practical religion, of applied religion, will set in. The world is crying out for a new type of Christian, ardent in faith and love to his Master, and therefore devoting himself, whether in or out of Holy Orders, as Christ did, to bearing and healing the infirmities of others. I know what noble work young clergymen can do and have done in Lancashire.

There is one branch of work in this direction to which perhaps a clergyman is specially called, and for which he has special opportunities : I mean to form, or present, a comprehensive, synthetical view of social questions. He is presumably a man of some general education. He ought to be able to master the interdependence of the varied social, educational, and religious questions, so as to keep them collectively before the minds of his people. He will find men who will give themselves to specific branches of the work. Let him try to make men realise how all are connected. He should be a moderating influence against one-sided views, but a stimulating influence for progress as a whole.

And there is another class at the other end of our social scale, which is at least as much demoralised by self-indulgence and aimless luxury as the poorest are by their poverty. And their demoralisation profoundly affects all the middle class—all of us. We ourselves individually have been and are affected by

the general indifference and hostility to any
legislative measures on a comprehensive scale,
for improving our public-house and licensing
system, and for controlling the drink traffic ; for
dealing effectively with the housing and land
questions, which are so closely connected with
other curses of the great cities. Nothing
excites more furious dislike than any attempt
to interfere with men's vices, unless, it may be,
an attempt to curtail their profits. But it is
not only those whose profits or pleasures are
involved who disclaim any sympathy with the
aspirations of the labouring class for a more
human home ; it is often the religious and semi-
religious middle class who appear to grudge any
rise in the standard of life in the class below.
The general attitude of Christian people to
social work and progress is very unchristian.
We must be perfectly well aware that we
ourselves find it very hard to maintain our
faith in any ideals for national life ; that we are
infected by the apathy of the leisured class;
that the most ardent reformers of national life
do not usually regard either clergy or the
leisured class of Christian people as their

natural allies.   Until we realise that our
apathy and aloofness are a sin, of which we
need daily to repent, among the things we have
left undone that we ought to have done, we
must be regarded as foes, not as friends.

Now you must get to know and to feel the
national peril and distress, not of course in order
that you may be always taking part in political
and municipal agitations, but that you may be
saved from the sin and shame of drifting,
through social sympathy with the unawakened,
unideal class to which you belong, into an
ignorant, contented indifference, or even active
hostility, to the aspirations among the best
and the few for diminishing these evils.   Our
profession is not the slightest guarantee against
this sin and shame.   It was not the clergy, as
a rule, who urged the protection of little
children against overwork in the mills half a
century ago, or who have agitated for reform
in unhealthy trades, and in the conditions of
labour for women and children.   Most of the
clergy in the southern states of the United
States of America up to the last defended
slavery.   Remember that we may be as blind as

they, and bring no less disgrace on our office. It is one of the dangers of our profession that we should be more in sympathy with the social conservatism of the well-to-do than with aspirations for bettering the conditions of life of the poor, and that we should let subscriptions blind our eyes, lose sensitiveness to moral wrongs, and be cowardly in speaking of them.

When I speak of a true and inspiring theology as the only force capable of counteracting the degrading forces constantly at work, I am not thinking of the theology of the professor, but the theology of the ratepayer and taxpayer and newspaper reader, the average popular thought about God. It is this that ultimately determines the trend of public sentiment and action, and it is this which it is our special duty as pastors and educators to purify and elevate and strengthen. We have to translate theology into the language of the people. The result is pastoral theology.

Wherever a strong and simple thought of God, and of God's relation to man—that is, a strong theology—enters into a man's mind, and through him seizes on a body of men, or a nation, it has a directive and compelling effect in bringing all their aims and purposes and wills into line with one another. Such thought acts like a magnet on a box of iron filings; they leap into position, they transmit its power. Out of disorder arises order, out of particularism unity. The wills of men are then ordered, directed, marshalled, by an attraction towards an Unseen Power—a religious ideal. Such is the result of a theology. There is no such co-ordinating power in the world as this.

To give one instance only, I will take the theology of Mahomet, that prophet, mystic, theologian, soldier, who arose to scourge the degenerate Eastern Christianity of the seventh century. His intense conviction of the nature and will of God filled his whole being, and its precision fascinated and convinced the men of his age. He and his caliphs were irresistible. It was their theology that tipped their spears with steel. Had not creed met creed, theology met theology, with a faith and chivalry equal to their own, Mahometanism would have overpowered Western Christendom. Theology determined social progress and

world - history in those days. It is equally
powerful now.

Now, must we not say that the popular
English theology of to-day is degenerate, or
almost evanescent? Have we not as a
nation, in our ordinary business life, come
to think God so remote as to be negligible?
Have we not as a nation settled down to
the belief that, for all practical purposes,
we are left to our own devices; and that
God educates us, as some one has put it,
by leaving us strictly to ourselves? It is this
negative theology, this *laisser-faire* theology,
which makes possible our silent acquiescence
in conditions which are so fearfully unfavourable to all higher life. The degradation of
character that comes with inability to find work,
the slums of a city, the wasting weariness of
unhealthy trades, the yearly massacre of children, the savage indifference of us all to the
welfare of those who create our comforts, are
all tolerable to such a no-theology as this,
but are intolerable to a real belief in God.
Can any one doubt that this no-theology is
the theology of the nation, and that the utter

weakness of this no-theology is the cause of the absence of any high ideals of national life?

Now, here our first thought may be: "Yes, this is the theology or no-theology of the *nation*. But it is not the theology of the *Church*. The theology of the Church, some one will say, always has been, and still is, the great agency for purifying and elevating that no-theology of the nation. That is our *raison d'être*. Our work as clergy is marked out for us: it is deplorably ineffective, we admit; but we can only follow on the lines so clearly and authoritatively laid down in the Prayer Book, and leave the result to God."

Here we come near the root of the matter. It is not possible, I think, to over-estimate what Christianity did for us in the earlier ages of our national history, under very different political and social conditions. It was the one restraining force, the one source of ideals of life, the one influence that kept the spiritual world before men, that defended the weak, that awed the strong. It was the uniting influence in the nation, as well as the training, the ennobling, and the educating influence. The

Church was the soul, the conscience, the poetry, the art, the home, the school of all the ideals of the nation. The very stones in its ruins cry out that they owe their undying beauty to the faith in God which inspired their building. But can we say that it is so now? And if not, why not? We must face this question. If we look impartially at its more recent history, we shall not be able to maintain that the Church, even in its widest sense, along with a continued influence for good on individual life, has to an equal extent determined or inspired the ideals of modern social and industrial evolution. Surely we must acknowledge this. We have great resisting, but comparatively little inspiring, power. The Church of England in particular has great dignity, a splendid position; but we must recognise that this dignity is due to bygone historical causes, and that its splendid position was given to it because of its splendid service under other conditions. Civilisation has perhaps done more for the Church, of late years, than the Church has done for civilisation. But this need not be always so. "He that doth serve" becomes

great; and our greatness can only be maintained by " service," and by the full recognition
of all who " serve."

There surely is a new ideal urgently needed
—the ideal of industrial and commercial life.
Into this life all the masses of our people are
swept. Religious life cannot be kept apart
from it, and confined to our churches and our
personal devotions. Industrial and commercial
life—yes, and the life also of recreation and
society — must be penetrated with some
Christian ideal, if the kingdom of God is not
to be regarded as a mere dream. Our pastoral
work brings us face to face with this life, which
is, however, entrenched behind a barrier, and
most difficult to touch. Pastoral theology must
find a passage through this barrier, unless it
is to acquiesce in its impotence. We suffer
from cowardice, from ignorance, from unwill-
ingness to touch difficult subjects. We suffer
also from the prevailing use of seventeenth-
century English in religious teaching. It
seems to be thought that the language of the
clergy, like their dress, ought to be different
from that of other people. It is this that is in

part responsible for the divorce of religion from
common life.

Our lack of inspiring power is, however,
primarily due to the prevalence among ourselves of an unworthy and feebly-held theology,
which has enfeebled and dissipated our wills
and aims; and if the Church is once more to
affect social progress, it must begin by purifying
and ennobling its own theology, and thus
generating the force of love and self-sacrifice.
We have to go to the very root of the
matter.

The conception of God the Father as a
supreme Transcendent Being, as Ruler and
Judge, has in the past too much concentrated
men's thoughts on His absolute power, confused men's sense of divine justice, and lowered
their sense of human worth. It created, as we
feel (for we too are affected by this theology)
an infinite gap between God and ourselves,
and presented Him to us as complacently contemplating human misery in this world and the
next. Wherever the doctrine of God's absolute
power and transcendence is held predominantly,
it lowers man's respect and hopefulness for

man. The thought of such a God overpowers
and numbs the mind. It tends to make men
first fatalistic and acquiescent, and finally
materialistic and unbelieving. Suffering and
misery and sin come to be regarded as God's
will. Even the work of the Redeemer in
popular theology has scarcely corrected this.
His work of redemption has been represented
as a transaction in the Divine counsels to save
a fraction of a humanity utterly lost ; and men
have thought they did Christ the more honour
by glorifying the vengeance of God, and magni-
fying the sinfulness of men. I cannot doubt
that such a theology, which has long been at
the core of the popular thought of God, has
retarded social progress by diminishing man's
hopefulness, by lowering his sense of dignity,
and his responsibility. It at once took away
man's power and motive for work, and made
men less worth working for ; and we are at this
hour suffering from this double paralysis—a
paralysis of spiritual energy, and a paralysis of
hopeful motive. Men's minds have been wholly
diverted from the Messianic hope of a kingdom
of God on earth. This is the reason why so

much of the virile mind and heart of the country is outside our Church and all Churches.

I know it may be argued that this is not the theology of the Church ; some one may even be found to say that it never was the theology of the Church. But it is the theology which the people have learned from the Church. They have mastered and absorbed but little, but they have mastered and absorbed this,—that according to us our chief duty is to get to Heaven, and that there is some easier way of getting to Heaven than by doing the will of God and loving our brother. We are, indeed, quite willing to love our brother if it costs us nothing—even if it can be done by proxy for a small subscription. But our teaching has not culminated in brotherly action. We have lent ourselves to this illusion, or acquiesced in it for want of clear insight into something better.

Now, I believe this to be a passing phase of theology in our national history, in which generations are but as days in a man's life. It is not the theology of Christ ; it is not the vital part of the theology of the Church ; and it rests with your generation to prove that it is not the theology of the true teachers of our Church; but the fact remains that this is the residuum which has survived in men's memories when the rest, which many of us try to teach, is forgotten. Brotherliness, to sum it up in that word, is forgotten, because it is but a purple patch placed on a system which seems complete, and has been taught as complete, without it.

Let me then try to give you some outline of what I think is the theology of Christ and His Church, the universal theology of the future, if not of the present—the theology which is nevertheless directing, though often unfelt and unformulated, some of the great tidal social movements of our time, largely outside Church influences—the pastoral theology, in a word, in which I find my hope for England, and which I would fain see inspiring every class.

To put it in briefest form, Christ teaches us to honour and respect every man as in some sense an embodiment and a potential representation of the Divine. Theology at its truest testifies to human worth and human capabilities. It is all summed up again and again in St. Paul's phrases, but they seem almost to have lost their meaning to us by repetition, and by the overpowering prejudice in favour of a theology which almost overlooks them. What does St. Paul mean when he speaks of the "one God and Father of all, who is above all, *and through all, and in all*"? What does he mean by saying that "to each one of us is given grace according to the gift of Christ"? or by speaking of this mystery now at last made known, of "Christ in you the hope of glory," and his hope to "present every man perfect in Christ"? or of Christ being "revealed in" himself? If these phrases, and many others, like coins long worn, have lost their original impress, and are now mere tokens, it is our duty to remint them, to fill them with life. And not only they, but the whole New Testament enforces this teaching—that man's worth is infinite, just because he is the child of God, and has in him something of that Divine Fatherhood.

This was the theology that moved the first generation of Christians. And surely no illustration can be given from history of the effect of a theology on social progress to compare with this, the preaching of Christ and its effect on the world. Take what view men will of the nature of Christ, and of revelation, still this is undeniable, that it was a theology, a distinct doctrine about God, and of man's relation to Him, that inspired with passionate faith and feeling and love the early Christians, nerved them to efforts, to devotion, supported them in persecution and in what seemed hopeless combats with a world of evil. It was a theology that in this instance determined social progress, that put down the cruelty of the amphitheatre, the infanticide, the unnatural and bestial crimes, the slavery, the wrongs of women and children, and other evils of those times. It was theology: it was the thought of God as "the Father of all, above all, and through all, and in all"; as a loving Father; and of our own human race as His children in union with His Son. It was this thought that brought into line the noblest aspirations among men; and we cannot imagine that without such a theology such results could ever have been attained. If ever there was a pastoral theology it was this,

And what is of still more importance, it is this theology, formulated or unformulated, that is the moving force of civilisation and progress to-day. I believe that below all the dogmas of theology, among people who know nothing of dogmas, there are stirring thoughts which are strictly theological, *i.e.* express views as to the nature of God, and His relation to man. It may be ours as pastors to bring these thoughts to the birth, by giving them distinct expression. There is no nobler task. It is to bring out the latent religion of our democracy. This is the pastoral theology I commend to you. Surely it is this to which you are called.

And thus finally I come to the question what may be the effect of such a theology on social progress in the future—of a theology which spiritualises society by spiritualising and glorifying the human unit, and recognising it as united to the incarnate Saviour.

One of Carlyle's greatest sayings was that the conflict of the future lay not between the Tory and the Radical, but between the believers and the unbelievers. Similar sayings might

be quoted from Mazzini, Emerson, and many
others.

Think what a vista this opens. It means
that in the fullest sense, as Mazzini said, " every
political question is a religious question "; that
" not till democracy becomes a religious movement can it hope to carry the victory." It
means further that social evolution and progress are bound up with the prevalence of a
noble faith. Just so far as the English people,
as a whole, have a grand ideal of personal
and national life, an ideal necessarily and
inherently religious, so far will our progress
be steady and well directed and secure, in
making the life of the masses more worthy,
more noble, and more happy. Surely this
ideal should come from us pastors. What
we need is the acceptance of St. Paul's
grand and simple doctrine of " Christ in
men." I believe the world is ready to
receive it, and I believe the Church, in its
widest sense — " those who call on the name
of Jesus Christ our Lord" — is almost ready
to give it; and will give it when her eyes
are opened to the lack of power in all

they are expressed in terms of Greek philosophy, and cast in a mould unfamiliar to our age, there is found the truth we need, if we will but look for it.   We must not throw away the old, but see the new, which is really the oldest of all, the nucleus of all within.   The new will not come to destroy, but to fulfil.

The faith in the Incarnation is more than a belief in the Divine Sonship of Jesus Christ; it is a faith that human nature finds its goal and consummation in Christ, and is even now and universally a potential manifestation of the Divine.   " Beloved, now are we the sons of God, and it doth not yet appear what we shall be."   The historic faith in Christ as the revealer of God in His words and works, in His all-sacrificing love, is not a worn-out faith, but one full of power at this day.   If we are all to be brought into line, with a passionate desire for social progress, and an enthusiasm that burns up all jealousies, it will be by the love of Christ, the personal love for a personal as well as an ideal Christ, filling all hearts.

And the faith in the Holy Spirit is the belief that the impulses towards goodness which we all feel are a link to God Himself, and spring from a source other than, and yet working in, our own personality. It is this that gives power, and patience, and toleration, and mutual respect. This wonderful world of men is the sphere of the Spirit, and we must beware lest we be found fighting against God.

Therefore, in conclusion, it is to the theology of to-day, purified of lower and mistaken views of God, simplified, intensified, penetrated by scientific thought, that I look as the main engine and power for social progress. No mere mutual struggles inspired by selfishness will make a world of love; no checks or counterchecks will eliminate dishonesty and tyranny and oppression; no shuffling of dirty cards will make a clean pack. No mechanism of institutions and societies; no education by codes and systems, can effect anything without the fire within. It needs the inspiration of an ideal from without to direct and co-ordinate human effort towards a noble end, and this ideal is nothing else than a noble pastoral theology.

Have faith in this ideal, in the universal presence of the spark of divine life. Some day these sparks shall leap into continuous flame, and then the kingdom of God will have come to all.

What a work lies open to the pastoral theology of the future! It is not merely national progress. It is to win for Christ the leadership in the philosophical thought and practice of the world. It is assuredly true that the thought of our new century seems to be moving away from the belief of the last century, that in the study of physical nature and her laws all mysteries could be solved. Everything, our poetry, philosophy, science, literature, converge on man as the being in whom the answer to the riddle of the universe is to be found. Such too is the teaching of theology; that it is in man, regarded as the child of God, rather than in nature, that we are to look for the purpose of creation; and theology adds that if in man, then most clearly in our Lord Jesus Christ. If we clergy are now faithful we may do something: we may help to draw the nation's eyes to Christ as verily the Way, the Truth, and the Life; and what nobler, what more patriotic aim can we put before ourselves than this? In such pastoral theology—that is, in philosophy applied to the supreme problem of bettering human life, and expressed in language that can be understood of all—lies the great motive power of human progress. It is to this pastorate that you are called.

LECTURE III

ABSTRACT

The importance to the Church of the study of philosophy.

Every pastor should be acquainted with the existence of philosophic and scientific difficulties, though he cannot acquire the knowledge required for dealing with them.

Some of these general difficulties and problems stated.

What ought to be the pastor's attitude towards them.

We may rightly abstain from speculative questions.

The need of a sound and strong basis of theology, supplemented by some knowledge of science.

Special points in which scientific knowledge directly influences our teaching. The transformation of transactions into processes, *e.g.* the Creation, the Fall.

A few words on miracles.

What science has done to strengthen faith.

III

THE PASTOR'S ATTITUDE TO PHILOSOPHY AND SCIENCE [1]

IF lectures on pastoral theology are intended to assist in the preparation and equipment of the young pastor in his work, at least one lecture should be devoted to advice as to the spirit and intellectual temper in which we pastors ought to face those speculative difficulties which are associated with science and philosophy.

We are not all called on to deal directly with apologetics; but all of us ought to know something of the great obstacles to faith, and of the way in which those obstacles may be, in part, at any rate, overcome. They are not

[1] These lectures were in print before I had the advantage of reading the valuable article, "The Present Attitude of Reflective Thought towards Religion," by Prof. Henry Jones, in the *Hibbert Journal* for January 1903, and the *Life and Letters of Dr. Martineau.*

matters for the amateur to deal with offhand.
A very slight acquaintance with the subject
shows that the success of all opposition to
Christian faith depends in no small degree on
the literary and philosophical ability with which
difficulties are presented; and the success is
often increased by the weakness of unskilled
defence.   Most of us had better leave the
defence in the hands of men who combine philosophical training with faith, such as the late
Aubrey Moore, Illingworth, Inge, the Bishops
of Manchester and Worcester, Hastings Rash-
dall, and the late J. Caird, and others.

Beyond this general advice I cannot go.
These are not lectures on philosophy in general
or on the philosophy of religion.   You must
look for these elsewhere.   I will only say here
that no one can profess to be a scientific theologian without a good knowledge of philosophy.
Useful pastoral work is done without a knowledge of philosophy; but such a pastor must
not venture far into the field of scientific
theology.

But I will very briefly indicate what I mean
by speculative difficulties associated with science

and philosophy. And I would add that I do this solely in the hope of showing that a strong, masculine, and reasonable faith is perfectly compatible with the frank recognition of these unsolved difficulties, and in the hope of giving you courage to take your own pastoral line. Difficulties in some form have beset every age, and our difficulties are after all the heritage and the characteristic problem of our time. But they will not in their present form last for ever, and they must therefore be regarded as a part of the Divine purpose unfolding itself in the evolution of the race.

Most of us, I hope, have had some training in physical science; or, if not, we have at least lived in an intellectual atmosphere of which scientific principles and methods form a part. If this atmosphere has really affected us, we find it, on the one hand, impossible to limit to the material world the application of these convincing principles and effective methods; and, on the other hand, if we impose no such limitation, and if we are at all logical, we seem to convert mind and soul into purely physical phenomena, dominated by law and mechanism, and to refine away the distinctions between men and animals, between animals and vegetables, and between vegetables and minerals, and thus obliterate personality.   This is, in general terms, one of the characteristic difficulties of to-day.   We can draw no line between the material and the spiritual, and we can make no harmony between them.   We can neither divide nor unite.   There appear to be insuperable difficulties in thinking of nature as sharing in life, or of ourselves as isolated and discontinuous spots of life in a non-sentient universe. Perhaps we have to learn how important differences are, even if we only think them to be differences in degree.

We are, again, led by scientific methods and tests to limit real knowledge to the results of our experience of the finite; but we are none the less unable to give up our convictions as to the infinite as a necessity of thought.   Here again no unity, no synthesis, seems as yet possible.

We live in another respect also, as it were, between two worlds, one dead, the other "waiting to be born."   What are the criteria of

theological truth ? the principles of theological
criticism ? We can neither justify a creed nor
dispense with it. The age of instinctive, un-
questioning faith, a faith wholly independent of
philosophy, has passed away from some of us,
and we seem to be endeavouring to restore it,
or replace it, by philosophy. But philosophy
has never yet replaced religion ; and to endeavour by philosophy to revivify faith is like
trying to galvanise a dead body to life.

Religion seems made up of unreconciled
antinomies, of points of view which suggest
theories that we cannot reconcile. The problem
of heredity and circumstance and self-deter-
mination is ever with us ; that of necessity
and free will is never far off. From one point
of view, religion wholly consists in identifying
our wills with God's will by living in mystic
union with Him ; from another, it wholly consists in rightly discharging our temporary
relations with one another.

More particularly at the present time we are
called on to face the most delicate of all
operations—the separation of the essential from
the non-essential but traditional elements of

G

the Christian faith.   There can be no development, no growth of an organism, except by the
passing away of something.   Our age is one of
growth.   Ought we not to regard this as a
privilege rather than as a misfortune?   But
what is to pass away?   What is permanent, or
relatively permanent?   What is transitory, and
"ready to vanish away"?   To take one illustration—what is the final importance to faith of
events recorded in time?   Are historical events
to be for all men and for ever the foundation of
ethics and of faith?   Does the sanction of the
Decalogue, for example, as a rule of ethics
depend now on the historical narrative in which
it is framed?   Or has the Decalogue at length
acquired another sanction in the ethical nature
of man, which it has so greatly contributed
to awaken, and to which it is a permanent
witness?

We see and teach now that it is wrong
to steal, not because stealing is forbidden by
the Eighth Commandment, but because the
Eighth Commandment, viewed in the light
of experience, has helped to disclose the moral
fact that it is wrong to steal.   We see and

" know of our own selves." Is it possible that the Christianity of a future age will be similarly based on something in addition to its historical basis,—on a spiritual consciousness, on an aggregate experience of a sonship to God, which, through the historic Christ of the Gospels, shall have become part of the inheritance, and one of the axioms, of the world? Of the two testimonies, " the Spirit itself " and " our spirit," that together bear witness that " we are the children of God," is the *onus probandi* being slowly shifted to the latter? And if this is possible, are we already witnessing, in some of the spiritual movements of our time, the throes that precede the birth of that age? Now, all this is the subject matter of philosophy; and therefore the Church cannot dispense with philosophy. The gravest and most practical problems, moreover, of our time are the philosophical problems arising out of evolution, heredity, determinism. It is to philosophy we are to look for guidance in education, in legislation, and in administration of justice; in all the questions of socialism, and property, and public duty.

These are outlines of some of the speculative difficulties round which the thoughts of
religious men are now revolving ; and nothing
is more necessary to the well-being of the
Church than that some among its pastors
should be masters of philosophy.

If, however, it were the duty of every pastor
to attempt to deal publicly from the pulpit with
these and similar questions, then few indeed
would be qualified for Holy Orders.   It is
emphatically the duty of all who have the
requisite ability.   But it is not *our* duty unless
we happen to have quite exceptional gifts.   It
is, however, our duty thoroughly to realise that
these questions exist, and that there is nothing
unfaithful or irreligious in entertaining them.
It is part of our duty to sympathise with and
respect those for whom these questions are
intensely real, and to acknowledge that we
cannot at present and alone resolve these
questions : and lastly, it is our duty to make it
clear to ourselves how, without intellectual dishonesty, we can leave these questions aside
as not in our individual sphere, and do our
own work modestly but whole-heartedly, a

true pastors of our flock.   We must not limit
the ministry either to philosophers, or to those
who see no unsolved problems of faith, and have
no philosophic doubt.

You must, in the first place, convince yourself of the inestimable value of all knowledge,
and vow never to join in, or even to tolerate,
the attempts of the ignorant, the timid, or the
intolerant to disparage it.   This must be your
immovable attitude, even when knowledge, as
it grows, seems to alter all the proportions of
your existing faith.   How wrongly, as we stand
on the path at the bottom of some Alpine
valley, do we judge the distances and heights
and groupings of the peaks far in front of us !
How incessantly and surprisingly do we modify
our first judgment after reaching fresh points of
view !   There is an analogous error, and an
analogous correction of error, in the world's
judging of spiritual things.   We, of all men,
must be priests of truth : for God is truth, and
every truth won by man brings man nearer to
God.   Truth is that ethereal region in which
the human holds intellectual communion with
the divine.   It is easy, perhaps, to say this,

but history shows how hard it is for religious
men to hold this truth fast.   Convictions
ought to be strongly held, but held with a
mind open to fresh intellectual light.   How
knowledge has poured in on the world !   God,
who has taught us so much, has surely more in
store for us, and we cannot in the least foresee
of what sort it will be.   We all acknowledge
the progressiveness of revelation in the past ;
we, of all men, must open our minds to the
revelation of the present, and "harden not our
hearts."   The God whom we serve is a living
and ever-present God.   Man is not yet what
he shall become.   We have faith that he will
at last cross that

> Gulf dimly divined
> Between the living world we see
> And the world as it ought to be.

And the next thought I wish to impress
on you has been well put thus: "I have
been led to conclude that perhaps the religious
systems of all countries are now more or less
an attempt to uphold the unfathomable and
unconscious instinctive wisdom of millions of
past generations against the comparatively

shallow, consciously reasoning, and ephemeral conclusions drawn from that of the last thirty or forty." This is a striking way of emphasising the truth that, whether our existing philosophical systems can embrace it or not, faith in God, and in a spiritual kingdom of which we form part, is a necessary and ineffaceable part of human nature. We need not be in the least perplexed if some system-makers tell us with reference to God that "they have no need of that hypothesis." *Securus judicat orbis.* Our pastoral work lies not with men engrossed in any scientific or philosophic system, with minds preoccupied, but with people who have for the most part wholesome and natural religious instincts; and I think the author I have just quoted says somewhere that "reason uncorrected by instinct is at least as dangerous as instinct uncorrected by reason."

It will be noticed that I have said nothing here of the pastor's attitude to historical studies. It is because this needs nothing less than a whole lecture to itself.

There is surely nothing more important to

us than to know what Christianity really is; and we can only learn what it really is by ascertaining from the veracious and scientific study of history what it has been. That veracious and scientific study of history has begun, and from it, as from the studies of philosophy and science, and perhaps even in still larger measure, light will pour in upon theology. The past has been for the most part held up to us not as the material from which reason may extract some guidance as to the evolution of the human race and human mind, but to illustrate and recommend some theory. The true study will doubtless raise many questions, as well as solve many. The theology that may result from it will not be exactly the theology of to-day, but it will rest on so broad and assured a basis that the generations to come will not tremble at the name of historical criticism.

It is by such reflections as these that most of us have to justify our abstention from speculative questions, even while we recognise their existence. Our pastoral work, in the immense majority of cases, lies with those who are incapable of entering into the region in which scientific difficulties arise. They cannot analyse their religious belief. They hold the spiritual truths of the Gospel by the grasp of healthy instinct and right action. Experience is to them sufficient verification of those truths. We are not all of us called to the study of apologetics for dogma; and there is a large region of opinion outside that of positive dogma, in which truth will only result from discussion. But we may not be called on to take part in that discussion.

We cannot make it too clear to ourselves that the real bond of communion in the Spirit of Christ, into which we desire to enter along with all our people—and no one will deny that this is the highest aim we can put before ourselves—is not at all the bond of a common philosophy, or of a common education, but that of a common spirit and aim—a humility, a simplicity, a Christ-like temper, a life like that which we may suppose Christ's to have been before His public ministry, which we may share with the humblest. Intellectual pursuits, if allowed to absorb the thought of a pastor, and

unbalanced by the completest sympathy with
the common life of all men, separate him
from his people. It is the bond of a common
earthly and of a common spiritual life which
unites, and there lies the sphere of the pastor.
That bond is completely symbolised in the
Holy Communion, in which is set forth the
equal capacity of all for participation in the
divine life, and for fellowship with each other.
Never for an instant let us admit that the
sphere of our work is of an inferior order,
because it cannot be treated on purely intellectual grounds. It cannot be depreciated
and disparaged by such phrases as that clergy
are dealing not with truths but with sentiments,
not with facts but with fancies—that we are
content with illusions. We must and we can
claim that there are whole regions, and those
the very finest, of human nature which lie
outside intellectual definition and intellectual
conviction, and yet, as has been said, " they
give to conviction much of its practical vitality
and momentum." " Great thoughts come from
the heart." There is a standard of value
other than the intellectual; and we refuse to

submit our work to an intellectual standard of value alone.

And if we are taunted with accepting illusions, let us reply that there are illusions and illusions : that we will uphold no illusions bred of an unveracious optimism that desires to conceal unpleasant facts; but that the religious view of the world, bringing out its beauty and its sublimity, even though we " see in a glass darkly," is no such illusion. The world is something great and glorious, and anything which helps us to appreciate its greatness and its glory is not of the nature of an illusion, but is an interpreter of fact. Religion is the highest poetry of life : it admits to the region of reality.

I am no philosopher, but I imagine that a philosophical reply might also be made to this charge that we deal with illusions. The charge is usually made from the side of physical science. But there are differences as well as resemblances between the methods of establishing truth in physical science and in religion. All knowledge implies the subject and the object, we are told; but the externality of the object

varies from the complete externality in the
material sciences to the very attenuated externality in the personal experience of our inner
life. Knowledge in the latter case cannot have
the same external tests, and the same external
verifications, as in the former; but it is not
therefore an illusion, though it may be deemed
so in the judgment of one who from a limited
range of thought takes physical science as the
sole standard of knowledge. I believe that
the universal application of this standard is
already becoming a thing of the past, and will
ere long be as much a curiosity of philosophy
as scholasticism.

But though the sphere of pastoral work with
our people lies apart from these philosophical
problems, for our own sakes we need more
than a popular theology as a foundation for our
convictions. We need, if you will, an esoteric,
as well as an exoteric, theology. The two will
of course be identical in every respect but that
of expression. But the expressions may differ
very widely. Just as a doctor has his scientific
diagnosis, which involves conceptions utterly
unknown to the patient, or as a physicist has

conceptions of physical action which he transforms in the attempt to popularise them, so
the pastor ought to have behind the popular
theology which determines his expression, a
deeper set of theological principles which co-
ordinate and consolidate his own thoughts.
The doctor will talk of infection and fever;
but he is thinking of bacilli, and phagocytes,
and I know not what. The theoretic elec-
trician will talk of currents and induction; but
his mind dwells on the unexpressed mystery of
the ether. There must be something closely
analogous to this in the mind of a good pastor.
He will speak of Father, Son, and Holy Spirit;
of the soul, and the final judgment, and the
eternal life in Heaven; but he will know that
not to him or to any man is known, except by
imperfect analogies, the ultimate reality of the
subjects of which he speaks. He will remember, though his people do not know, that
by the nature of the case our words express
limitations arising out of our own limitations.
"Without a parable spake He not unto them,"
must be as true of the servant as it was of the
Master. Not the loftiest thoughts that man

can attain to can be adequate to express God.
And this knowledge will make the pastor
humble, sincere, reverent; and the humility of
his knowledge will knit to him the simple
hearts of his people. He will always speak
as in the temple of the Unseen God, and
he will avoid the familiarity with which the
unthoughtful preacher too often speaks of God,
to the offence of some, and to the vulgarisation
of others, of his hearers.

There are further reasons why every pastor
should acquire such knowledge as he can of
scientific and philosophic reasoning.

We cannot fail to note that among men,
along with a growth of confidence in Christian
ethics as the necessity for national life, there is
a lessening interest in theology and Christian
evidences. Among the uneducated class,
there is a growth of spiritualism and its
impostures; and among the educated classes,
there is marked alienation from Christian
thought, and in some cases the growth
in its place of fantastic beliefs, — strangely
concocted pseudo-science and credulity. We
cannot help asking why this should be. Most of

these men and women have been under Church teaching. Why has it gained so little hold upon them? It would be unwise to attribute so general a result to any one cause. But among the causes must be placed the very imperfect religious education which from our pulpits, and in our schools, we offer to our people. Reflect that in every other subject, in all places of higher education, teachers stimulate to the utmost the critical, and literary, and scientific spirit: they encourage activity, originality, and independence of thought. An education which does not stimulate the desire to investigate ultimate principles is rightly thought defective. And by these methods of teaching a strong sense of reality in all other branches of knowledge is given to our scholars. They see that it is based on experience.

But in teaching religion our methods are too often quite different. You may re-member, if you have read Ibsen's *Brand*, the description of religious teaching given by the Dean :—

> It's all so easy : Faith, you see,
> Broad-based upon authority ;

> Which being upon learning stayed,
> May be implicitly obeyed:
> While rule and ritual leave no doubt
> How faith ought to be acted out.

It is so precise and sympathetic a description of a method which we recognise as common that one might almost fail to notice that it is satiric.

This is one reason why the study of some one at least of the natural sciences is so desirable for clergy. It is not the additional knowledge that such a study gives, but a certain almost indefinable change of attitude. The old mediæval ideal of a university, which still haunts us, and in particular haunts the theological schools and colleges, is that of simply conserving and transmitting knowledge and opinion. It unconsciously assumes that truth is already ascertained, that everything is known, and that we have only to acquire it, and hand it down. Our faces are towards the past. But the study of science turns our faces to the future, to what is not yet known. Its attitude is always one of investigation, not of authority. It is always looking forward. Now there is an unconscious antagonism between these two types of mind. We preach in vain to men who have learnt that patient and modest investigation alone will win truth, if we are not so far in sympathy with them in their own subjects as to understand their attitude. Our teaching even of religion should have an experimental note in it. It should rest on verified facts, and look for still further light to be cast on the faith.

We must lay much of the blame on our own shoulders for the alienation of people from theology ; we must recognise that something is wanting in the education they get from us. And this is a very real reason for our endeavouring to study, a little more profoundly than used to be necessary, the difficulties of religious faith.

But it is time to turn from these generalities on the influence of scientific thought on faith to some particular points in which scientific knowledge must directly affect our own popular teaching. Its effect may perhaps be described by saying that it has in many instances transformed a transaction into a process.

The dramatic conception of God fashioning

the world and all that is in it in six days, and
resting the seventh day, appeals to the poetry and
the imagination, and it stimulates the religious
awe of man in presence of the supernatural.
In the absence of any suspicion of proof to the
contrary, it was quite justifiable to ask, Why
should it not be a fact?   It was a very ancient
belief; it had been purified by Israel of much
of its grotesqueness; it lent itself readily to
moral uses; it was indeed a splendid parable;
it had some apparent relation to the common
facts of observation; and it had become part
of our orthodox belief.

But this dramatic conception is gone—
vanished from the educated world.   It has
gone, and yet it has left no vacuum behind.
We have learnt within a few generations that
this earth is not the centre of the universe; that
the six days' drama is poetry, not science—the
dramatic representation of a process as a transaction; and we now know that we have no
other means than scientific investigation for
finding out how this earth has come to be what
it is.   But we are sure that it was a process,
continuous in the main; we know that it is

very imperfectly understood; and that there is no proof that there were not discontinuities, as there is no proof that there were. The main point is that Creation, which used to be taught as a transaction, is now seen to be a process.

You may fairly ask, when, to whom, and where, am I to interpret Creation as a process, and how connect this teaching with the drama of Genesis? I have still in my ears the indignant words of an old secularist, spoken at a public meeting convened to discuss difficulties in the Bible: " How long have you gentlemen in black known this and concealed it from us?" I think we little know how much conflict of faith and reason, and how much distrust of the clergy, so obvious and so painful in recent controversies, is due to concealment of such truth. My own belief is that in every pulpit, whenever the subject is touched on, we should make it clear that the early chapters of Genesis are but the pious cosmogonies and speculations of the ancient world, which we prosaic Westerns have too literally interpreted as an inspired revelation of scientific fact. No boy or girl above our infant schools should be left in ignorance of our knowledge. Nothing should be taught which must soon be unlearnt. Every fossil in the school museum cries out against literal teaching. But still the old argument is heard in the workshops: " The churches teach lies—they teach that the world was made in six days."

Has the Fall quite ceased to be regarded as a transaction, and become a process? It is presented to us as a dramatic transaction. There is the serpent, the tree of knowledge of good and evil, the woman, the man. How are we to teach it? We are doubtless individually convinced that it is not a miraculous event in actual history. It never took place in the way in which it is recorded. The hold the story has on us lies in its truth to human nature, and in its wonderful imagination. We see it before our eyes. Such was the parable under which some inspired teacher of old imaged to himself the inexplicable fact of the incompatibility of sin with human nature as we know it ought to be. We know in our hearts that the Fall is a process repeated in every one of us and in the race. A man falls not once, by one insane act of folly, but by countless acts, and loses his

Paradise, and then the flaming sword turns him back on every side. I cannot put the positive teaching better than it has been put by the late Professor Hort. After saying that it is no longer reasonable to assume the account of the Fall to be strictly historical, he goes on : " But the early chapters of Genesis remain a divinely appointed parable or apologue, setting forth important truths on subjects which, as matter of history, lie outside our present ken. Whether or not the corrupted state of human nature was preceded in temporal sequence by an incorrupt state, this is the most vivid and natural way of exhibiting the truth that in God's primary purpose man was incorrupt, so that the evil in him should be regarded as having a secondary or adventitious character. Ideal antecedence is, as it were, pictured in temporal antecedence." It will be a great step gained in religious teaching when every day-school teacher, as well as every clergyman, may teach the story of the Fall with perfect honesty, because he may also, when-ever he thinks fit, teach that it is a parable.

In these narratives, then, and probably in

others, as in the story of Sinai, we are witnessing in our day the transmutation, under scientific
influence, of narratives of transaction into parables of process. To this transmutation our
minds should be fully open. It is going faster
and farther with others than with ourselves.
And the transmutation does not seem to be
even a temporary loss; it is an immediate
gain. But we must remember that unlearning
is a dangerous process, unless it is accompanied
with learning. The former is not in our con-
trol. But to ensure the latter, the perception
of the spiritual and eternal truth, is our duty.
The fact of the intrusion of sin against our
better nature; the need of struggle against
sin with every aid that discipline and medita-
tion can give us; the experience that sin bars
happiness; that we are in God's image, though
sinful, and find in Christ the renewal in ourselves of that image—these are the truths men
need not unlearn. And these are the truths
for the pastoral theologian.

These lectures are not the place for any full
discussion on miracles, and on our pastoral
duties in speaking of them. But the subject is

so closely connected with science and philosophy that it cannot be wholly left out.

The present position is this. There is
absolutely convincing evidence that some
events, which we should commonly call miraculous, as related in the Gospels, did actually
happen. I have given elsewhere [1] a full
treatment of this evidence. A chief point in it
is that in the undisputed letters of St. Paul to
the Corinthian Church, of which we know the
circumstances so well, he speaks of miracles in
the most simple and natural way, as having
been wrought by himself among them quite
recently. It is evidence one would accept in
letters of Cicero or of Pliny. I cannot doubt
that St. Paul's power of mind and will over the
minds and wills and bodies of others was so
abnormal as to deserve the name miraculous.
But then comes the *a fortiori*. What was St.
Paul compared to our Lord? The Gospel
narratives are less attested historical documents
than some of St. Paul's Epistles ; but if miracles
were absent from the Gospels, how should we
have accounted for their absence? That the

---

[1] *Essays and Addresses.*   Macmillan and Co.

"slave" of the Lord Jesus should have had
these powers, and his Master should have had
them not, would be incredible.

But in the next place, it is not necessary to
deny that an element of legend has mixed
with the narratives of the New Testament as
well as with those of the Old Testament.
Legend, however, is not quite the right word.
The story of a miracle was as natural and
obvious a way of teaching as was the parable.
It was teaching by picture; and the attitude of
mind towards such teaching was not among
the original hearers, and should not be among
us, either precisely to accept as fact or to deny
as fiction. The thought about such teaching lay
in a region equally remote from fact and fiction,
and disposed them to open the mind quite un-
critically, like that of a child, to the spiritual
influence and lesson of the story.

Further, it is perfectly impossible, on any
grounds, critical or other, to say that our faith
as Christians demands that one narrative shall
be taken literally and objectively, but that we
may think as we please about another. This
is, I know, a common solution; but it is only a

temporary one. I believe the subject to be, like many others which are much discussed, one which can never be settled, and one on which a settlement, even if it could be arrived at, would be of little importance. Not thus does Christ now draw the world to Himself.

Hence I think the true conclusion for us is that we ought with full intellectual conviction to express our belief that our Divine Lord possessed and showed powers far beyond our normal human nature, and thus showed His divine Origin and Being; and that while this demonstration is part of the purpose of those powers, there is always associated with their exercise a spiritual teaching, a revelation of an inner truth of things, which it should be our main duty to interpret. To insist on materialistic details has become a hindrance, not an aid, to faith, and diverts us from the main purpose of those powers.

Our thoughts in connection with miracles turn of course to the miraculous birth and the physical resurrection of our Lord. On these great subjects I do not think that the final

word can be said by our age. But in our
thought of the Incarnation there should be
one element always present to separate it
toto cœlo from every anticipation of it in other
religions. Other imagined incarnations have
been poetic dreams of men lifted above the
normal conditions of human life. The Greek
gods were but men and women lifted up
into the ether of the divine and then wor-
shipped. But the Christ whom we worship
lived under all the conditions of human life, on
this hard earth's surface, in a small and de-
spised nation, as infant and boy and toiler for
daily bread, and as suffering all our sorrows.
The Incarnation shows the ideal to lie not in
a region of fancy, but in our common life, in
our parishes, among working folk, in the
commonplace. This is no poetic fancy; it
is the eternal revelation of the divineness
and the dignity of all human life. This is
the secret of the power of the Gospel on
human hearts and human minds. It has
uplifted the whole of human nature from the
bottom.

So our faith is that the union of the human

and the divine, towards the knowledge of which the world is tending, was made manifest in Christ. That union of the human and divine, that atonement of man and God, demands from us an identification of our will with God's will, and therefore demands from us all the discipline, the study, the willing service that shall assist in this identification. This is the goal of our pastoral work. Here is the synthesis, and the simplicity we need; and it is as far removed from self-deification as it is from Deism. It is on this goal, however far off it may seem, that we pastors must fix our eyes. The extraordinary extension of human knowledge, and of human activities, may make our work in this age more difficult, and make it also appear to be less pressing, because the limited capacity of men's minds is so filled with sectional and material interests that there seems no room for the larger and the divine. But we may be sure that though men limit themselves to the finite, man cannot do so. He is impelled by a nameless force in quest of unity and truth and God. We may admit that the problem and the mystery of things is for the present beyond us ;

but never let us admit that it is beyond the ultimate attainment of man, when he shall have attained to the stature of the fulness of Christ; and let us keep the path open; and verily for this, Christ is the Way.

LECTURE IV

ABSTRACT

THE ethics of religious conformity.

Pastors are pledged to follow the lines of the Church of England in their pastoral and priestly office ; yet some liberty permitted.

This lecture is on the attitude of the pastor towards the Bible.

The Bible the foundation of the science of theology ; its uniqueness led to the belief in its inerrancy.

The meaning of inspiration if the Bible is not inerrant.

The ultimate foundation on which faith rests if the Bible is not inerrant.

The interpretation and formulation of human experience, past and present; its relation to historical evidence for the origin of Christianity.

The attitude of the pastor to the higher criticism. It must be fearless. The natural dislike of suspension of judgment even on minor points must be overcome.

The transference of authority going on at the present time.

The pastor's use of the Bible in teaching.

IV

THE ATTITUDE OF THE PASTOR TOWARDS THE BIBLE

In the two preceding lectures we have been thinking about the pastor's attitude towards national life and progress, and towards the scientific and philosophic methods and spirit. Now suppose some one says, " These questions are determined for you by two authorities, the Bible and the Church. You are not in a position, as an ordained pastor and priest of the Church, to act and think freely on these subjects. Your duty is prescribed for you once for all : you have surrendered your freedom ; you have to ascertain what these authorities say, and their mind and their system must be henceforward yours." What are we to say ? Is a pastor bound to act and think in fetters ? So we come to the subject of this lecture, the attitude of the pastor to the Bible, and to the subject of the next lecture, the attitude of the pastor to the Church. A few general remarks must precede.

There is no doubt that the popular conception of the pastor is that he is one who in taking Holy Orders sells his intellectual birthright and franchise, and becomes, once for all, the agent and minister of a book and a system. That is the feeling of many educated laymen towards us.

And there is no doubt that there are very many within our Church who regard with suspicion the Churchmanship, and even the Christianity, of any one who questions anything which they themselves accept unquestioningly; and that there are many outside our Church who resent as a dishonest evasion any demurrer as to the reality of the narrow restrictions they imagine to exist on the thought of the clergy. The nature and extent of these restrictions are therefore matters which need consideration. They influence, and often deter, men who contemplate Holy Orders. One who has been ordained with no clear thought about them must sooner or later consider them. The Ethics of Religious Conformity are a serious branch of Ethics.

Now in the Office for the ordination of Priests there are put before us, in true proportion and subordination, firstly, the aim of the pastoral and priestly office in the Church; and, secondly, the methods by which we pledge ourselves to try to attain that aim. "The office and charge to which we are called is to be Messengers, Watchmen, and Stewards of the Lord; to teach and to premonish, to feed and provide for the Lord's family; to seek for Christ's sheep that are dispersed abroad, and for His children who are in the midst of this naughty world, that they may be saved through Christ for ever." This work of bringing our people to the knowledge of the Lord Jesus Christ is, you will observe, put in the forefront; to bring them to Christ, to shepherd them for Christ, is the supreme and reiterated aim. The ethics of our conduct must be judged by reference to this aim.

Then follows a description of the methods that we propose to use. We will "minister

I

the doctrine and sacraments and discipline of
Christ, as the Lord hath commanded, and as
this Church and Realm hath received the
same"; and we pledge ourselves to be "dili-
gent in reading the Holy Scriptures, and in
instructing out of them the people committed
to our charge."

There can be no doubt that in these words
we pledge ourselves in general to follow the
methods of the Church of England and of the
Bible in doing the work of our pastoral and
priestly office. We are not entirely free and
unfettered evangelists. We will use the
Church's doctrine, sacraments, and discipline.
We will teach out of the Bible. It is in determining what degree of freedom is permissible
in adapting our methods, as pastors, to the
supreme aim of bringing men to Christ; in
discriminating between what is essential and
what is variable in loyally following our Church;
between what is the permanent teaching, and
what the passing interpretation of the Bible,
that differences of temperament and knowledge
and judgment come in, and make the question
one which has no definite and final solution

for us all.   History shows that interpretations
change and pass away.   There is *some* limit to
our allegiance to the letter of Church rules and
of Bible texts, though the limit is not clear.
We may well believe that men who truly love
and honour our Master with humility and a
single eye to His service, even if they differ
widely on this point, will not go far wrong.

The right attitude, moreover, for one man
and one age is not necessarily the same as that
for another man and another age.   We have
no ground for thinking that the divine ideal for
man is uniformity.   Life means variety, and
life is what we need.   I think, therefore, we
must conclude that, though the pledge we take
is real, there is nothing in it which tends to
reduce us to the level of mechanical agents of
a routine.   There is freedom under the pledge.
There is nothing to justify men in saying, as
a man once said, " I carry out to the letter the
Church's system, and if it fails the responsibility is not mine."   I need not tell you that
in his case it did fail, and I need scarcely
suggest that the only part of the Church's
system which he carried out was the mechanical

part of it. I hope you will understand that the last thing that the Church desires from you is a servile adherence to anything that can be called a method. We need some men whose fiery loyalty to the Master oversteps the conventionalities of His service, whose love of souls finds new modes of expression. The Holy Spirit is not bound to one method. New conditions demand new methods of warfare.

But I must come closer to particulars; and as a matter of convenience I take first, as the subject for this lecture, the attitude of the pastor towards the Bible, leaving for the next lecture the attitude of the pastor towards the Church. Indeed, the Bible is the foundation of the whole science of theology in a sense which has no parallel in any other science. It is not Christianity only, it is the whole conception of religion as the outcome of a revelation made by God in the hearts of men, that is involved in our thought of the Bible. The whole Bible from beginning to end assumes and contains this progressive revelation. The thorough acceptance and understanding of this point is therefore of the first importance to a pastor.

It is, of course, the plain and familiar historical fact that the Christian Church was in full life and in partial organisation before there was a New Testament. The New Testament is the product, not the charter, of the Church. But the Bible expresses the vitality of the Church, contains its fundamental beliefs, and will ever remain the source of our knowledge of the soil from which it sprang, and of the supreme Personality of our Lord, and of the spirit and thoughts that animated His first followers.

But, indeed, it is not a mere question of priority in time between Bible and Church; for it is historically true that it is from the study of the Scriptures that, in every successive age, a new awakening of the divine Life in men has arisen, recalling those awakenings which gave these Scriptures birth. Their revelation is perpetually renewed. The Bible is verily the Word of God in the hands and on the lips of the pastor. No words are too strong to express the difference in degree, as verified by human experience, between the enlightening and searching power of the books of the Bible and that of all other works. This is why they

are of such undying value. The fact finds its
verification in far too many hearts to be dismissed as a passing instance of human illusions.
There is a mystery in it beyond the reach of
rationalism.

The books of the Bible do not all stand
on the same level. We may approach them
naturally, and read them like other books. But
no one with an eye for facts can deny the
uniqueness of their power in the aggregate
over the minds and hearts of men. Wherein
this power consists is as difficult to define as to
say wherein consists life in an organism, or
genius in a man. We know that power by its
effects, as we know life and genius by their
effects. The power of the Bible is unique as
an inspiration to holiness and righteousness;
unique in its evoking in men's hearts the
consciousness of the divine, the call to the
higher life of the Spirit within, the temper
and character of the Christian.

But this uniqueness became, as we all
know, stereotyped into the mechanical theory
of an inspiration that made the book infallible
in matters of fact as well as in those of prin-

ciple. The Bible thus became the final
authority on every subject it touched. I perfectly remember, for example, when Darwin's
Descent of Man came out, that the question
was asked with bewilderment in clerical circles,
" How can a book be written on this subject?
We *know* how man was created." I do not
doubt for a moment that this intellectual form,
which reverence for the Bible and the feeling of
its power assumed, was a necessary stage in the
evolution of religious thought; it was like the
hard husk that protects the tender life of the
seed. These beliefs do not arise by accident.
The Church of England, indeed, meaning
thereby for a moment its authoritative documents, has never, as we all know, made this
infallible accuracy of the Bible, in either fact or
doctrine, an article of faith. But this was the
chief and unquestioned article of popular religious faith up to a generation or two ago; and
it is the survival of this popular religious faith
with which we pastors have sympathetically,
tenderly, but truly and progressively, to deal.
There lies the real difficulty—to help the error
to unfold itself into truth. And for this,

modesty, piety, sound critical knowledge, a
sense of the proportion of things, aptness to
teach, and above all a true pastoral spirit, are
our safeguard.

Two questions arise : the first touches the
nature of Biblical inspiration.   I said that our
Church of England has never made the infallible accuracy of the Bible in either fact or
doctrine an article of faith.   This is, of course,
not true of the Church of Rome.   Pope Leo
XIII., in his recent encyclical on the study
of Scripture, formally declares that "those
who maintain that an error is possible in any
genuine passage of the sacred writings, pervert
the Catholic notion of inspiration, and make
God the author of such error."

This perhaps fairly expresses the popular
belief among the less instructed of our own
people.   And it is worth our seeing into what
evasions any one will be led who attempts
verbally to retain this belief, and yet to face
the facts of Scripture.[1]

---

[1] See *Clerical Studies*, by the Very Rev. J. B. Hogan, S.S., D.D.,
published with the *imprimatur* of the Archbishop of Boston, U.S.A.
chapter xii. Art. (4).

He may be led, as some of us are led, to say that all matters of fact, historical or scientific, were left to the writers' human faculties, and are therefore liable to human error; but that in all spiritual matters the writers were infallible. This, however, is incapable of proof, and satisfies no one. Or he may be led to an evasion of the truth, by reading into the words some meaning wholly foreign to the mind of the writer, whenever he appears to contradict historic or scientific fact.

Let us avoid all such finesse and evasion. The true foundation of our interpretation must be to teach that the oriental habits of expression and thought of the writers are not affected by their becoming channels of divine teaching, and must be studied; that the scientific lines of demarcation between fact and allegory and poetry were not defined to them in literature as they are to us; and that even the closest union of the soul with God, the most inspired and saintly life, is no protection from errors of fact. The main contest with popular infidelity will turn on the Bible; and woe to us if we deal with it dishonestly. The birth of the historical spirit and method

like that of the physical sciences, has had, and
will have, a profound influence on the spirit of
Biblical study.   Let us be sure that edification
rests on truth; that the better we understand
the Bible the more it will be to us.   This
principle is of the greatest importance in
determining the character of the religious
education to be given in schools.

And it is by no means only in matters of
history and fact that we are bound in loyalty
to truth to admit errors in the Bible.   It is of
even greater immediate importance that we
should teach that the early ideas of morality
and of God were defective.   "We can no
longer say," says Aubrey Moore, "'It is in the
Bible, approved or allowed by God; therefore
it is right.'"   We must never allow ourselves
to forget that we are studying imperfect records
of a progressive revelation, and can never
spare ourselves the effort of a moral judgment.

But I must pass from this, which is now a
fairly familiar subject,[1] to a question far harder,
which is pressing even now.

The harder question is one which we

---

[1] See *Why Men do not believe the Bible*.   Two lectures.   S.P.C.K.

scarcely dare ask ourselves: "On what ultimate foundation is our faith to rest, the inerrancy of the Bible having disappeared?" It
is time for us to face this question. Is there
any answer, or only an uncertain one, made
up of qualified, hesitating, and contradictory
statements? It is for want of this answer that
many men dare not take Holy Orders.

Rome has an easy answer: "The Church
is infallible." And there are temperaments
impatient of suspense, who resolve to accept
this; and there are people whom this answer
in its crudest form will satisfy. But it is not
the answer of the ancient and Catholic Church;
and it is not true.

The answer which in our hearts we know
to be true is that, in God's scheme for the
education of man, there is no infallible authority
anywhere. The divine message on every
subject comes to the world of men through
fallible channels; we can never spare ourselves the pain and responsibility of judging.
Nothing is infallible. A living man may, as
we see, have the Spirit of God in him, and
evoke that Spirit in others, and yet be neither

sinless nor infallible. So books may be, and are, the vehicles of a divine message, and yet be very fallible.

It is to the totality, the consensus, or ethical judgments, to the collective spiritual insight of the best men, that we must look. And though the religious temperaments and sensibilities and capacities of men differ so widely, it is no discordant, uncertain result in which this consensus finds expression. There exists a voice of the universal divine, latent or germinant in the heart of every one—a voice of every age; and that this voice should ever grow clearer, more commanding, seems to be the purpose of the moral evolution, the spiritual teleology, of man. The inner and universal experiences—those convictions that lie so deep in our human nature that words do not express them, and ratiocination cannot formulate them—are the ultimate foundations of our religion. Our theology partly consists in the interpretation and formulation of human experience. Is it too much to say that our belief in the Incarnation is ultimately based on experience as well as on history? Experience is doing more and more every day to make credible facts both in the physical and spiritual world, which are lightly dismissed as fiction by those who have not studied the facts.

But do not human experiences vary, and will not our theology vary with them? Yes, just as continents rise and fall by secular changes; and yet it is not misleading to say that "the round earth standeth so fast that it cannot be moved." There is an immense continuity of human experience, like the submerged continents out of which islands rise; and this is the final authority of faith, the voice of God in the universal heart of man.

Now to say this is not to say that the historical evidence of the origin of Christianity has become valueless, or even secondary—still less to say that the teaching and preaching of Christ as the Saviour and the Divine Son of man is superfluous. "Do we make void" history "through faith?" Quite the reverse. "Nay, we establish" history. The evidence stands good, and is of primary importance. The study of the Bible known as higher criticism is meant, we must remember, solely to ascertain the historical facts, and the circumstances attending the origin of the various books, so far as is now possible. There is another, and a quite different question, which is not a subject for literary criticism, but is a subject for the philosophical and religious interpretation of experience—how far, and in what way, these books, whatever their origin, contribute to the elucidation of our human life and destiny on earth, and to the evoking into consciousness the Life of God within us.

As regards the first point, the results of criticism, I shall be extremely brief. You and I are alike unable to follow the course of the long and very extensive campaigns in the wide veldt of literary criticism of the last half-century. No man, however wide his learning, still less any one who is engaged in pastoral work, knows the whole field which is being explored by experts and specialists. But you may safely take it as established that the books of the New Testament are authentic records of Christian faith and thought as they existed at a very early date. That is as far as

history and criticism can take us.   The books
demonstrate that such and such was the belief
about Christ's life; such and such the thought
about His person and revelation and teaching,
and about the significance of His life and death;
such and such the order and discipline and
faith of the Society that sprang up to perpetuate
His life on earth, in the years that immediately
followed.   The Gospels are not interpretative
after-thoughts.   And that is enough for us as
pastors.   For if history and criticism go so far
as to demonstrate this, they make it certain
also that there was a historic foundation for
those faiths and opinions, and on this foundation, the historic Personality of Christ, we also
may rest.   That marvellous Personality is, or
may be, better known to us than He was to any
age between the first century and the twentieth.
And it is He who is our Life, and the Author of
our faith.   That is the solid positive result of
historic criticism.

We shall not be distressed by questions
whether St. Matthew was the scribe or the
source of the first Gospel, nor as to the relation
of St. John to the fourth Gospel.   No critical

question as to the objectivity of certain narratives should provoke us to take our stand here,
or draw a line there, and declare, " Thus far
and no farther shall the tide of criticism flow."
It were madness to make a doubtful point of
history or of literary judgment into a vital point
of faith.

Let me give again an illustration given
before.   On what basis does the authority of the
Decalogue now depend?   Is it on the objective
and literal truth of the narrative of Sinai?   Is
it on this in any degree?   We are compelled
to answer, No, it is not so now.   Whatever the
authority was once, whatever the interpretation
was once, it is now based on the collective ethical
judgments and experience of men.   And the
transference of this authority, at the hand of
criticism, from one basis to another, has not
weakened that authority; it has only disclosed
its security and solidity.

We may have watched as children some
workmen clearing out the soil close to the
walls of our house, and feared that the house
would tumble down; and behold, the house is
not built on the soil at all, as we thought, but

on a rock, whose existence we never suspected, which was covered by the soil. "Which things are an allegory."

So the right attitude of the pastor on points of Biblical criticism, as it seems to me, is that of intelligent, interested, and open-minded observation. It is not only that except in a few points we do not know much yet of positive results, nor that there is an element of time in establishing any result. There is such an element of time; for however confident one may be that something is proved or disproved, one must always allow for the possibility of fresh discovery, and for the illuminating thought of a new genius. But the important point is that we pastors must realise and teach that all questions of fact are to be dealt with by the calm discussion of evidence, not by authority. We may be sure that such discussion will show at last the real foundations of the faith we need. There is, I know, a hot-house faith that is cut down by the chill wind of criticism, but that faith scarcely seems akin to a divine ideal. Rather let our faith be robust enough to flourish in that biting air, and in the rough world of facts, and to draw strength from them.

But even this does not quite bring out my conviction. It seems to me that any one who allows himself to fear what may be the consequence of knowledge of facts, is in a very real sense setting up an idol, a false god, and deliberately bowing down to it. Facts are the expression of God's will; our opinions and preconceptions are the image we make of God's will. Which shall we worship? Can we hesitate? We shall, of course, be careful in weighing evidence, because great issues hang on the result; but we will not weight the scales beforehand by invincible prejudice or fear.

I do earnestly press on you this attitude of mind. If at its centre our creed was a temporary sham and an imposture, which we pledged ourselves to defend as long as we could, then we should do well to evade and postpone criticism. As it is, we have more than any one else to gain from truth.

Some one will probably suggest that my advice is tantamount to saying that the only reasonable attitude is to treat everything as an open question; that one cannot avoid agnosticism, but one must conceal the fact that one is an agnostic. Let us consider this, and begin by remarking that this is not a very accurate use of the word agnosticism.

There are some people so constituted that anything seems better than what Bacon calls the *adulta suspensio judicii*. Let their creed be extensive and definite, they say, no matter how shallow. It is this type of mind which classes as sceptics all who are not traditionalists; and, moreover, often calls them not sceptics but infidels. Such men are always in evidence. But this temper springs from impatience, and sometimes from unsettledness, or even insincerity, with a leaven also of irreverence. Is it not irreverence that is so ready to assume that all God's dealings can be apprehended by our small understandings, and that our generation can master all truth? And is it not impatience and insincerity to grasp at, and profess as satisfactory, a faith that does not satisfy the reason, and think such a profession a merit? This impatience of suspense is a grave temptation and danger to-day to the clergy. If a man does not hold some things more strongly than others, he holds all feebly. Suspension of judgment on a great many points is not infidelity to God; it is humility, and fidelity to truth. See whether such a suspense affects conduct, and life, and spirit. "By their fruits ye shall know them." Let me say at once that I hope we all know our ignorance on some things, and are waiting for more light.

> Think not thy wisdom can illume away
> The ancient tanglement of night and day.
> Enough : we acknowledge both, and both revere ;
> He sees not clearliest who sees all things clear.[1]

But the attitude of mind I am putting before you with respect to criticism leads to a very different goal on all the great essential articles of our faith. It is historically certain, a fact confirmed by criticism, that those who came under the personal or very close influence of Jesus Christ, no less than we who to-day study His life and teaching, have been alike unable to think of Him as an ordinary man. We are compelled, as they were compelled, to think that in Christ God Himself appeared as on

[1] W. Watson.

with human nature, and manifested the possibilities of humanity as He has done in no one
else.   And as a result, we feel it, as they felt
it, the only suitable, the only true way to speak
of Him as the Son of God, and the Saviour;
a man, and yet other than men; possessing
and revealing a spiritual power in man far
beyond the limit known to our personal experience—a power still seen to be as real as when
He was on earth.   All this is positive enough,
dogmatic enough for use.   There is no require-
ment laid on us to accept any speculative propositions about Him.   We are to take Him
into our hearts as the Life of our spirit, and to
realise our mystical union with Him.   "Our
profession," we are told, is "to follow the example of our Saviour Christ, and be made like
unto Him."   The Scriptures lead us to Christ,
and then they have done their part.   The men
of Samaria, after they had been brought by the
woman to Christ, said to her, "Now we believe,
not because of thy word, for we have heard
Him ourselves, and know that this is indeed
the Christ, the Saviour of the world."   Our
faith, in like manner, rests on no secondhand

evidence; it rests on experience, on an experience evoked by our knowledge of the historic Christ; and this experience is an evidence ever renewed, ever growing in cogency.

I have spoken at considerable length, because this process of transference of authority from the text of the Bible to some other centre is one of present importance and of some obscurity. The impatient pastor will seize at some semblance of outward authority, and pin his faith to some party or society; and when the illusion fails him, nothing remains but an unsettled despair or a blindfolded advocacy. Another type of pastor, patient and humble, accepts unquestioningly traditional views, but is too much occupied by work and spiritual experiences, perhaps too much engrossed by inward realities, to feel any need to revise his faith from an intellectual standpoint. One might well envy such a one, if it were not for the knowledge that his work as a pastor will be seriously limited by this curtailment of his intellectual sympathies. Such a one will be effective with those on precisely his own plane. But he will scarcely have the strong grasp of truth that will make him a pastor to those who are not on his own plane of this generation, or to the leading spirits of the next.

It is the attitude of the pastor, the teacher, that I have been speaking of. In his personal and devotional use of the Bible he should feel more and more its unique power of bringing him into God's presence, of laying open, uncovering, his soul to the sunshine and fresh air of heaven. If he studies the New Testament with modern lights, Christ ought to become very real to him—so real that he is helped to see all spiritual experiences of himself and others as with the eyes of Christ. The Bible is in this sense also the source of pastoral inspiration, the source of unity and solidity in his faith.

A very few words must be said as to the pastor's use of the Bible in the pulpit. The use of the Bible in the Day and Sunday School is equally important, but on this I cannot now speak.[1]

[1] May I refer here to a *Series of Notes for One Year's Sunday School Lessons*, which I have edited for the S.P.C.K.

There was an age of Christendom, not so
many centuries ago, when few people could
read, and there were no printed books. What
was the preacher's work then ? The subjects
of preaching were probably limited to the
Creed, and the narratives that bear on it, to
the Commandments and the Lord's Prayer,
the seven great virtues, and the seven deadly
sins. That is, the priest gave oral instruction
on the most important truths of ethics, of
Gospel history, and of revelation, and directed
and stimulated the devotion of a non-reading
public. Preaching, in a word, was ethical
and disciplinary. And the pastor spoke with
authority, arising from the mysterious powers
he was believed to possess. The selection of
the most important truths lay with the priest.
But with the Reformation and with printing
arose an almost universal and eager study of
the Bible, and the conviction that it was to be
interpreted by each man for himself. Teachers
and taught, clergy and laity, studied the Bible
with intense eagerness ; a new Protestant
eclecticism, and a new Protestant system of
theology, were the result.

The traditions of that age are with us, but the age has passed away. The Bible is now extremely little read in any class. There are survivals of the old homely domestic reading of the Bible, but they are only survivals, growing rare as old folk die. At this day it is a quite unfamiliar book in cottage and villa and hall. It is unique, it is honoured, but it is not read. It never before was so profoundly studied by scholars; but I believe it is less read for devotional purposes than it was at any time during the last three centuries.

The recognition of this fact must affect the preacher's use of the Bible.

To define how our pastoral use of the Bible is being affected by this unfamiliarity with the Bible is not easy. If one had to sum it up in a paradox, I should say that it is leading us to put our text at the end instead of at the beginning.

Instead of saying, " These are the words of the Bible, and therefore they are true and authoritative; and therefore such and such must be our belief, and our conduct," we are, as a matter of fact, largely reversing the

process, and saying such and such is the
verdict of experience as to conduct, such
and such the feeling of our hearts, such and
such is true; and we find that the most
fundamental principles of that conduct which
experience shows to be right, and the pro-
foundest expressions of those feelings and truths
which command our loyalty, are to be found,
with an unrivalled fitness of expression, in the
texts of the Bible. The wider our experience,
the more human and noble our thought—it is
already there in the Bible. Our philosophy is
indeed widened by all sorts of knowledge of
which the writers of the Bible had no conception; but feeling is deeper than knowledge,
and it is their feeling, their spiritual insight,
which inspires us to interpret our own feeling,
and to see how all our new knowledge deepens
that feeling. Most of all, we find that the total
ideal of human life and conduct, and of man's
relationship to God, is expressed in Jesus Christ.
He therefore becomes the end, the goal, to which
we lead our people; in the light He sheds on
human life, they tread on solid ground of experience all the way, and find Him at the end.

This teaching lays stress not on authority, until the authority has been accepted by the heart; it lays stress on experience, and shows how it vindicates authority. Moreover, it lays stress on those elements in man which are common to us all, not on that which is individual, whether it be learning or feeling or mode of life. Below all our differences of knowledge and ability, all our varieties of temperament and capacity for imagination and emotion, and all the infinite grades of occupation and industry, is the universal human soul. That is the sphere for the pastor; and his study of the Bible, not as a theologian, constructing a scheme, but as a man and a lover of men, will draw thence for him large draughts of human sympathy. Thus viewed, the Bible will ever be growing more and more to us and our people, and we shall find the old words true fact: "The testimony of the Lord is sure and giveth wisdom unto the simple."

LECTURE V

ABSTRACT

THE danger of professionalism, and the attitude of the pastor towards the Church.

The justification for part of what is considered professionalism.

The necessity for a strong feeling of Churchmanship.

What it implies in our aims.

The welcome we should give to variety; the effort needed to cultivate wide sympathies.

The attitude of the pastor to the neutrals in a parish, especially of the labouring class; to the thoughtful class who hold aloof from our creeds; and to dissenters.

Our attitude to the National Church, as regards conformity in ritual and doctrine.

The ethics of conformity briefly considered.

The new theology which we may welcome.

The new theology, or philosophy, with which we can make no terms.

The mission of the pastor in contributing to religious philosophy.

V

THE ATTITUDE OF THE PASTOR TOWARDS THE CHURCH

I have been speaking of some of the causes which may altogether deter some men who possess truly pastoral qualifications from taking Holy Orders, and which probably affect you all to some extent.

I have spoken of the uncertainty as to fitness : the doubt whether the ministry offers at the present day a good field for social and moral usefulness. There is the hesitation arising from the fear that for a man to take Holy Orders is to commit himself irrevocably to opinions which further acquaintance with philosophy or science might render untenable ; or to a view of the inspiration and authority of the Bible which he no longer holds ; and now, lastly, there is with others an aversion to professionalism—the fear that ordination will compel a man to adopt permanently the ecclesiastical or clerical way of looking at things, which is thought to be inseparable from the work of the ministry.

This last difficulty resolves itself into the attitude of the pastor, *quâ* pastor, towards the Church, and forms the subject of this lecture.

It is the most difficult theme of all, because such phrases as "the Church," "professionalism," "the ecclesiastical and clerical way of looking at things," are extremely difficult to define. But every layman knows how alien and unattractive the clerical attitude, as popularly conceived, is to the lay mind. I will not attempt to describe it, except by indicating in general the exaggerated value clergy seem to them to set on things relatively unimportant ; the bitterness and impracticability that they associate with all ministers of religion, when they touch education and politics ; and, to turn to a very different subject, the inconsistency of professing high unworldly ideals in the pulpit with exhibiting what seems very ordinary conduct and temper out of it.

I am not going to deny or extenuate, still less defend, our besetting sins. But I offer two remarks for consideration, and would remind such objectors, first, that in the world as it is, a high degree of onesidedness in emphasis is necessary to secure attention to the spiritual, in presence of the urgency and clamour of the material; still more, if any reformation of conduct or revival of old truths, or any recognition of a new duty or truth, is to be effected. It is difficult, we know, to "be angry and sin not"; it is quite as hard to see clearly a great forgotten or neglected duty or truth, and not to press it out of season and out of all proportion. Such insistence is sure to be represented as exaggerated, impracticable, bitter, whether it is so or not.

And secondly, all these defects and faults are not characteristics of the clergy in so far as they are pastors, but in so far as they fall short of being pastors. For the true pastor can scarcely be a party man. The pastoral spirit is incompatible with party spirit; that is, it is incompatible with precisely those faults which the laity chiefly associate with the ministerial

L

profession.   This is seen to be true the moment
it is uttered.   *Quâ* pastor a man has no heart
and no time for the relatively unimportant;
one cannot associate the pastoral temper with
bitterness and impracticability, nor again with
worldliness.   " I have no fault to find with Mr.
So and So," is constantly the verdict of the layman on the clergyman who is first and foremost
a pastor ; and very many more of us are first
and foremost pastors than any one would gather
from the utterances of controversialist clergy,
or of those who dislike the clergy.

If then men fall into those clerical vices, it
is because to that extent they are not pastors.
I assure you that you may avoid all those unpleasant professional characteristics, on one
condition—that you give yourself to pastoral
work.   There is the best security against
clerical deterioration.

I am deprecating militant clericalism ; but
you must note that the absence of militant
clericalism is only a negative virtue.   It may
easily pass into the vice of deadly indifference,
unless it is combined with something that looks
at first sight like its opposite—I mean an ardent

conviction that a pastor can do little for his own people, except by strengthening among them the bond and the spirit of churchmanship; and that he can do still less for the people outside the direct influence of religious bodies, except through the faith and ministry and example of an inner circle of Church folk. His personal influence on his own people is transient and slight compared to the influence they will exercise on one another, if they are fused into one body, inspired and moved by the life of Christ consciously realised as living in them. In this sense the pastor, though not a party man, must be a very strong churchman indeed. That is his *raison d'être* so far as he is a pastor—to keep a flock together. He must idealise his congregation and his inner circle, and magnify their office. He must remember that they are verily the children of God, and members of Christ. Our own virtues, such as they are, could not be even what they are but for the stimulus of this membership; and if they are to grow greater, it must be from strengthening this bond of union, and from a fuller realisation of the brotherhood, the privileges, and the duties of the Church. It is as members related to one another, and in a joint relation to Christ, that each will grow. Every leaf on the vine is helped by every other leaf, as well as by the root. It was through the felt unity of Israel, as God's Servant and Child, that individual Jews felt their own sonship to God. Moreover, the realisation of a common life and interest in the Church widens people's minds, and prepares them for larger thoughts as nothing else does. It is an epoch in a person's life when he passes out of sheer religious individualism. His association with others multiplies the channels of influences upon him, and confirms his fleeting good impulses. People learn from one another. Public spirit and Church feeling are thus great educators. Their stimulating and mind-opening influence is remarkable. Worship, moreover, especially sacramental worship, scarcely exists apart from the common life which centres round a church.

It is only by association with others, indeed only by sacramental association, that the full characteristic Christian life can be realised.

One who holds this view, and sees that his own influence is only one factor in the total influence of the Church upon a man, will have an inner defence against the besetting professionalism.

Pastoral theology therefore teaches, as the result of experience, the need of a very deep loyalty to the Church, as the organ through which the divine Life in men finds its nourishment and its expression both towards man and towards God; and it teaches also the necessity of combining this deep churchmanship with perfect humility. Such a combination ensures a complete freedom from the mannerism, and temper, and priggishness, and still more from that occasional aggressiveness, which laity resent as clerical—from what I have called militant and self-assertive clericalism, the disagreeableness of which ranks high among the temporary causes that deter men from seeking Holy Orders.

Loyalty to the Church means the desire to strengthen the bond and spirit of this society in Christ as a great spiritual and educating force. This intelligent, convinced loyalty is a necessity to a pastor in his efforts to assist in the

development of character. But it must be a
great churchmanship ; it must be loyalty to great
aims, to great principles ; loyalty to Christ, to
His precepts, His example, His temper. Let
us teach our people the things which are great
in a true perspective—to be unselfish and even
self-sacrificing for one another ; never to speak
ill of others, or misrepresent them, least of all
those who differ from us in religious observ-
ances; let us teach them to be liberal in money
and service, as the tribute of their love to God
and man ; let us teach them to pray and discipline themselves by purity and self-control ;
let us help them to realise Christ and the Holy
Spirit in their own hearts ; " let us take care,"
as Jeremy Taylor said to his clergy, " that
we make our people Christians," and then we
shall find that they so love the prayers, and
sacraments, and life of the Church, that they
have become good churchmen. Let us leave
to controversialists who have not the care of
souls all curious and insoluble technical questions about " validity," and " succession," and
" authority." They do not concern us as
pastors : and let us never lay stress on

any points of Christian faith or worship or conduct as necessary unless they can be manifestly shown to be so, and are admitted to be so by the experience of men. To insist on distinctions, to exhibit the sectarian and exclusive habit of mind, is not pastoral. Be loyal to great aims, and educate the people towards them. No one has such opportunities as we have for correcting gradually the false perspectives, and the lower conceptions of religion, that are so common. You must not, of course, be always trying to "preach down" false or lower conceptions of God and of the Church by direct argument; but by dwelling on the vision in every heart of charity and the thought of social righteousness, and the kingdom of God among men, we silently doom those former conceptions to a painless extinction; we antiquate them; we relegate them to the unimportant. A few years pass: there has been no revelation, nothing startling; but the light has increased, and with it reality and piety.

Loyalty to these great aims, to the love of God and man, is at the base of the pastoral character; but there is room for large diversities

among us, which we must learn not only to
tolerate, but to welcome. It should be part of
our pastoral theology, as it is part of God's will,
to welcome diversity as a human characteristic,
reconciled, as it may be, by a higher bond of
union. Think constantly that all men are in
some degree manifestations of God; that all
good men have something to teach us of the
Infinite God. They are fragments, units, in
the vast total. "Nous sommes les chiffres, Il
est la Somme," as Victor Hugo says. From
every one something of His light is reflected.

This thought helps us to correct a species of
self-asserting individualism which implies that
no one else should be other than what we are.
What a poor, dull, unprogressive world one
type alone would make! The true idea of a
church, as St. Paul taught us, is the sympathetic
union in one body of very diverse members.
We forget this in practice. We are to feel
neither our own vigorous individualism, nor that
of others, as narrowly restrained by authority
or merged in routine; it is rather to be hallowed
by mutual respect and sincere humility, and
by fixing our thoughts on great aims. How

dare we belittle others? As Bishop Creighton
said, "With the cry 'Arise, shine,' sounding
in our ears, how can we waste time disputing
about the shape of our lanterns?"

I dwell on this point because I see how
much the influence of good men is limited by
their inability to enter into the varieties of feeling
and emotion that actuate others, and how this
fault of the clergy deters young laymen from
taking orders. It is unpastoral, it is even to be
called wrong, not to force ourselves to respond
sympathetically to the æsthetic, the symbolical,
the impressive ritual that appeals to the
emotion of some of our people. It may not
accord with our natural temperament; we may
have strong prejudices against it; but the fact
stands that a certain stateliness and dignity of
worship, with its historic associations and its
liturgic minuteness, appeals to some souls, as
nothing else appeals, and opens the gates of
the soul to the divine presence. We must
welcome this as one of the aspects of the many-
sided divine spirit in man. Not less must we
welcome those who can evoke the soul in their
hearers in the least ornate of services, by

passionate, though they seem to us unbalanced, appeals to the sense of sin, to the need of salvation, and to the redemption by Christ. Nor again are we to disparage others whose heart is so set on brotherliness, justice, and righteous dealing, that they incline to regard with impatience all efforts to secure precision either of ritual or doctrine. We, as pastors, must recognise all varieties of religious temperaments, and help them to understand one another by our own sympathetic understanding of all. Some of us may recall a striking sermon by Phillips Brooks on "Symmetry of Character," from the text "The length, and the breadth, and the height of it were equal."

And this large sympathy can only be attained by our loyalty to great aims. I emphasise this because I see our danger, and the harm this militant party temper does to the Church. We pastors have our own "world," from which we must strive and pray to keep "unspotted." Each of us has a "professional world," which is vehement for some passing phase of things; we play to a little applauding theatre of our own choosing, which exalts into principles what are really minor matters, and thus generates a temper in which the great message is forgotten, and in which men seem to have no words, no heart, no faculty for what is really spiritual and eternal. We must "keep ourselves unspotted from" this professional "world."

Again, loyalty to the Church is more than the uniting spirit of churchmanship in a congregation, and more than the sympathy for many types of religious mind which grows up with loyalty to great aims. It implies the right attitude of mind towards those who seem to us outside. The error into which, from a sort of excess of churchmanship, we are strongly tempted to fall is to regard the Church in any parish as coextensive with those who "go to church," and to regard all others as outsiders, schismatics, agnostics, or hostile. This is an easy line to take. And if the pastor thinks this in his heart, his congregation will make it plain in word and action that they think so too; and then there grow up the evils of Pharisaism, and the fold is henceforth fenced with barbed wire.

What are we to think of the many "neutrals"

in every large parish — the hundreds to
whom the clergy are simply nothing, and to
whom the expression of religion is unmeaning?
We must remember that God has so created
men and society, and labour and custom have
so fashioned them, that only a few are capable
of entering keenly into the feelings of devotion: the faculties of worship in most men are
nearly dormant; spiritual emotions have not
been developed in them. We know this perfectly well to be true from the experience of
periods of our own life. Let us honestly admit
this fact. They may be good men and women,
with a real loyalty to right, living quite as
good and decent lives as their neighbours who
go to church or chapel; but they have little
consciousness of the invisible, and no conscious
need of worship. They have no use, or very
occasional use, for church. Are these outsiders? or are they a part of our Church? Most
really a part of our Church. They have been
baptized; most of them know a little from Day
and Sunday school about the Bible and the Faith.
They can repeat the Lord's Prayer. Many
have been confirmed: they know the Christian

temper and Christian character as well as we
know it.   Perhaps they show it as well as we
do.   All sorts of reasons, good and bad, but all
at bottom the same reason, keep them away from
church—the limitations of faculties and temperament ; but they are a section of our people
not to be regarded as outsiders.   I want you
to regard these non-churchgoers with generous
and discriminating respect.   I am sure that
this way of regarding them will grow on you at
last, if you have the pastoral spirit ; but one
would like to anticipate the slow teachings of
experience.   There is something in the pastoral
work of a parish, in the daily contact with
labouring men and women, apart from all
churchgoing, that brings home the closeness
of Christ to our working and common humanity.
Jesus of Nazareth in the early years of His
manhood, before He was called by the Spirit
to His public ministry, was a working man
of Nazareth ; and His parables and teaching
show how familiar to Him were the details of
the peasant life.   Let us think of Him thus
at times, and not always as a person of the
Holy Trinity ; nor see Him always as a vision

of the Divine on earth; nor even always as the
Teacher and Healer and Redeemer. In this
thought of Him, as leading the homely life of
bread-winner, not then less the Christ than
when He hung on the Cross, we can see perhaps how labour was an element in His human
training; and we shall more truly respect the
worth of the hard hand, and the bent back, and
the shrunken figure, and the toil-stained face of
working folk, even if they come to no church.
The life of labour and toil is of the nature of a
sacrament. Grace comes to men through it.
It is a purifier of life. What dangers and sins
beset those who do not labour! These men
and women are not outsiders, because they get
their heavenward discipline in the stern fields
of labour, and are as yet all undeveloped in
their consciousness of the presence of the invisible; and are often, as it may seem to us,
terribly materialised by their limitations. That,
however, is not the materialism that demoralises
like the materialism of full-fed idleness. The
thought of the invisible, and a conscious loyalty
to Christ, can be only very slowly awakened
in them by much personal effort on the part of

some Christian man or woman.   But their lives
are wonderfully sweetened by such an awakening, and their humility is often an instruction
to their teacher.

There is also another class of men and
women whom we must keep in mind—who are
willing to accept Christ, but who do not accept
the Creed.   When that possibility first dawns
on a man it staggers him.   It seems impossible.
What does it mean?

It means that the Christ who is revealed as
a whole in the New Testament appeals to
men's hearts, and wins their acceptance because that sublime Personality is not out of
harmony with their ideal.   How should it be?
Christ is the eternal Son of Man, and the
eternal belongs to every age.

But such men can never forget that the
thinkers and philosophers and preachers of the
early centuries, from whom our creeds come,
not only accepted Christ as the revelation of
God and man, and as the atonement and hope
of the world, but they formulated what they
thought in terms of their own age.   And those
intellectual forms are of necessity passing,

temporary, relative.   Christ is eternal; creeds
have in them an element of the temporary.

The true pastor must have intelligent sympathy and deep respect for such men as these,
even though he fails to understand their difficulty.   Let us think how would Christ, the
pastor pastorum, deal with them.   These are
not wolves to be kept outside the fold.   Not a
few of them put us all to shame by the sincerity, humility, patience, devoutness of their
lives.   The Church fails of Catholicity till it
finds, not a place only, but an honoured place,
for men of this devout and philosophic and
faithful temperament and training.

And what shall I say of the pastor's attitude
towards dissenters?   On this I have a strong
opinion, based on experience and observation.

The simple fact is that there exists no sort
of bitterness between the church and chapel
folk in our parishes.   It cannot be fanned into
flame even by the fury of agitators.   If we
only read correspondence and articles in news-
papers, or believed what noisy political people
say on platforms, we should be hopelessly wrong.
Thanks   to   the   good   feeling,   the   common

Christianity of the masses, and the removal of inequalities, the real relation is unquestionably one of immovable friendliness. "We're chapel folk here, sir, in this house; but I'm glad to see you." "Sit ye down, sir, and welcome." That is the all but universal tone, when one calls at a house. So we have a talk; and it ends with the same friendliness as it began. "We're all going to the same place, I take it. I'll give you a look in some time"; (that means come to church). "Ye'll call again, I hope." That is the typical, almost the universal, relation between a pastor and his dissenting parishioners. There is no thought on either side of proselytising as conceivable. So my advice is to accept heartily their point of view; express and feel the most sincere hope that their chapel, Sunday school, and Day school give them what we all need. You may talk to them about Bible reading and prayer and the religious bringing up of their children, and, if it is opportune, you may pray with them. But never try to find out what they have been taught; never argue. It is simply the fact that "we are going to the same place."

M

It is the fact that, even apart from all family traditions, the more homely preaching and less liturgical methods and ministry of the chapel suit many of them better than anything we can yet offer. The attitude which is true to fact is to regard all as fellow-workers in the same Church: all are one flock, if not one fold. The actual separation between the congregations (apart from politics) has in it little or nothing of the temper of schism; and we must be extremely careful not to make schismatic in temper what is only in their eyes a difference in administration. All are our allies if they are helped by chapel to lead godly lives, to observe Sunday, to read the Bible, to avoid plain sins, and bring up their children well. By their fruits we know them. The Church to which a pastor of a parish must be loyal includes, therefore, the churchmen, the neutrals, the thoughtful outsiders, and the dissenters of his parish.

These last remarks about our loyalty to the greater Church lead me, to avoid misunderstanding, to speak next of our loyalty to the Church of England in particular. It is of that

Church that we are ministers; and it is within the limits of that Church, from first to last, that our activities must lie. We must not think that within those limits are found virtue and saintliness, and outside it, speaking generally, worldliness, ignorance, and superstition. To be a pastor in the Church of England means that we have chosen our path. Men can only work effectively by limiting their programme of action, and this is our limit. Our path is that of the Church of England. Who are we to judge others? The Church of England is large enough and good enough for us. We accept its limits. We accept its English, Anglican, notions and characteristics. If we are loyal to our national Church, our catholicity will take care of itself. Catholicity is not like undenominationalism, a residuum which remains when all that is individual is struck out. Just as undenominationalism degenerates into a faithless and lifeless kind of Unitarianism, or Theism, or less, from striking out every thought which is not equally approved by all Christians, so denationalised catholicity drifts into a mechanical mediævalism, galvanised for a while into activity, without its natural roots, and without its simple faith. Let us be loyal to that English catholicity, native to the soil and rooted in it, which the centuries have given us.

As pastors of the Church of England, we declare then our conviction that the union of our sheep in this fold of ours serves a high spiritual end; and that, from childhood upwards, in home and in school, and in all the cross-currents and storms of life, the faithful membership of our Church is a great safeguard and help to a good and pious life. The organisation of our Church in worship and teaching and sacraments is, we declare, to be our main instrument in bringing men to know and follow Christ, and to make their hearts the home of His Spirit. It is a net that can catch and retain those who would otherwise be homeless and isolated, and would lose those spiritual influences which ripen the soul. Our loyalty to our Church is based, therefore, on our experience and conviction of the disciplinary, educating, and inspiring influence of belonging to such a body as ours; on our seeing how it restrains from worldliness and sins; how it checks vulgarities and conceits and arrogances; how it creates humility and reverence and refinement.

But again this loyalty to our Church is much more than sentiment. It is a pledge of obedience. We pledge ourselves, as plainly as words can pledge us, to "obey our Ordinary, submitting ourselves to his godly judgments," "to minister the doctrine and Sacraments as this Church and Realm hath received the same." The attitude of promoting party aims, disregarding the judgment of the Bishops, is, however we may gloss it, a breach of our word and of our loyalty that nothing can justify. It exhibits the unholy and wilful temper of schism. We may desire more freedom and elasticity of services, and as Church reformers we may press for more, and we may use the very large liberty we possess. But we owe willing obedience to our Bishop, and all the more because disobedience rarely now involves legal penalties or pecuniary loss, and wins the admiration of the unthoughtful partisan. Such disobedience shows all the sinfulness of schism without its element of self-sacrifice.

And our relation to the doctrine and theology of our Church is governed by the same rule. We are equally bound to submit to our Bishop in the matter of teaching as of order. We are servants of the Church, of the Church of England; and to be servants implies humility and obedience. Our obedience and loyalty are due to the whole body of Christ. We are not at liberty to blurt out any views that for the time attract us and admit of some justification; we speak, indeed, as ambassadors of God, but also as messengers of the Church, and we may compromise others by our words as by our actions; and if this disloyalty is less injurious, it is only because few people understand words, and all can see actions, when they are disloyal.

The condition, in a word, of effective work is co-operation, and this condition is far too little realised among us. But co-operation implies willing self-limitation, self-suppression; it is inconsistent with the wilfulness of individualism, with the spirit, which, if unrestrained by the material bonds of money and position, would become schism. We have no right to claim and receive the benefits and pay of a Church to whose doctrine as a whole we are not loyal. To do so is not honest.

But in saying this we again open a very large and very difficult question, which can only be slightly touched on here, viz., the Ethics of Conformity. What are the limits of ethical freedom in continuing the use of fixed creeds and formularies, when we have ground for thinking that we do not use them either precisely in the sense in which they were used by those who drew them up, or precisely in the sense in which they are repeated by the uninstructed and unphilosophical members of our congregations? We must admit the difficulty that arises from our having to express our belief in the great truths of Christianity in their fourth or sixth century dress.

But there are counter considerations.

I can only offer a few remarks on this point. It demands separate and careful and full treatment.

(1) All language is metaphorical when applied to religious abstractions; and all such language is approximate, poetical, parabolic.

All such language has, moreover, a history. We do a grave injustice to the past, no less than to the present, if we think that the great thinkers and divines who drew up our formularies were blind to this fact, and infer that we must interpret all their words as prosaically exact. They also knew the imperfection of words.

(2) It is much more possible for a congregation to join in worship that is poetical and archaic in its language, than in one which is modernised and "up to date," and therefore to be judged and interpreted by either a colloquial or a philosophic standard. The mind engaged in worship is not analytical and reasoning; it is devotional, receptive. Worship is much more akin to poetry than to science, to art than to philosophy. Worship is, moreover, an act of the Church as a whole; and it is a result of its continuous life that the Church uses the prayers and creeds and hymns of its youth with a fulness of association and feeling that could not gather round new words.

(3) If any one tries to reduce to exact

statements the points in which fixed creeds and formularies embarrass himself personally, he will find how very few they are. And if it then occur to him that our Lord, in teaching as He did in the Sermon on the Mount, was at far more points in conflict with the old law, and yet described Himself as only "fulfilling" it, he will be disposed to concede that we may enlarge the interpretation of our formularies without contradicting them, and purify from what is temporary without destroying them. Our business is always to look at the spirit, not at the letter. The Church must have fixed terms of membership, which cannot be altered year by year; but it must also have the full freedom of growth and interpretation. It is death to prefer the letter to the spirit—death, as it was in Judaism to retain the lower sacrificial type of worship in presence of the higher prophetic type. We must have fixed terms of membership; but their interpretation must grow with our growth. Christ only demanded that men should follow Him, and we have no right to ask more. The creeds are as fences, given us to define the fruitful pasture, and to warn against wandering into the deserts. But they belong to the age of struggle and of imperfection. As our Church approaches its ideal, its creed will become more poetical, and approximate to a *Te Deum*.

It is the scientific mind applied to theology that frames the formula, and the scientific mind has its place ; but the mind of the mystic also can work within those formulæ, and must claim the right to interpret them, and in every age of the Church has done so. Moreover, we cannot think of God's knowledge as other than intuitive, unreasoned ; and it follows that the more closely our nature approximates to the Divine the more intuitive will become our religion, and the more religious our intuitions.

The continuity, moreover, of our Church is a continuity of worship, of sacraments, of ministry, of pastoral care, and of organisation, much more than it is a continuity of theological formulæ and opinion.

I may add that the fixity of interpretation of our formularies in our own Church, if it really existed, would be as fatal to truth and as embarrassing as the doctrine of papal

infallibility, only throwing the infallibility into
the past instead of the present. And if we
even pretend to fixity, if we regard any devia-
tion from past interpretations as of necessity a
step on the down-grade, and frown on and
denounce those who take it, we are guilty at
least of a strange confusion of ideas if we
remain members of the Reformed Church. A
Reformed Church must be a Reforming Church.

I claim therefore for the pastor, on all
grounds, that he may be utterly loyal to his
Church, and yet exercise in his conscience a
large liberty in the interpretation of her
formularies. It is not disloyal to the Church
to endeavour to find place in those formularies
for the new theology of the philosopher and
man of science, which welcomes the conception of a God manifesting Himself in all
historical religions and in all nature—in her
laws and uniformities, and especially in man ;
and welcomes therefore the mergence of the
natural into the supernatural, and can admit no
discontinuities as necessary. It is not disloyal
to welcome a theology which turns our faces
more towards social righteousness and the

bringing in of God's kingdom on earth, than towards our own individual salvation and the final judgment. It is not disloyal to welcome a theology which is at once more philosophical, more mystical, and more practical than the old, and read it all into the old prayers and creeds and liturgies. They are full of it, when we have eyes to see. We look for God more and more in the life of men. Perhaps our truest worship of Him is to share His love for all living things. All else is but the cloister of the temple, the approaches to the shrine: this is the Holy of Holies; and no words or symbols shall detain us as we press onwards to find God Himself. This is the temper of the newer theology, and should be the temper of the pastor.

This new theology that I have so briefly indicated is to be welcomed, and may be welcomed, with perfect loyalty to our Church. But it may not be amiss here to insert a word of warning, and to say that there is also a new theology with which, as far as I can see, there can be no compromise at all.

There exists a theology, or rather a philosophy, which practically confuses God with the world; it identifies them. Now it appears to me that the antithesis of the old theology between God and the world is true to human experience, and that in this respect the new theology is false. The truth of a theology, remember, rests solely on its correspondence with facts, its power of elucidating and co-ordinating human experiences. The newer theology admits duty, morality, righteousness, but has no place for grace as the action on man of the Spirit of God, no place for union with God, no place, we may almost say, for God at all. A theology which explains human experiences, hitherto regarded as arising from the action of the Spirit of God, as individual and unreal illusions and delusions is no theology, and should be called by another name. It should be called psychophenomenology. If Nature and Grace are not different, then there is no Grace: if Nature and God are identical, then there is no God. If, indeed, experience, broadly and fairly considered, should lead to this conclusion, accept it we must in the long run: *magna est veritas*. But the voice of

experience, to which we bow, points to an
external influence on man for which there is
no place in the " new theology."

I know that these lectures are not the place
for these discussions; but pastoral theology,
without discussing them, has perhaps the final
word to say on them. For it is simply the
fact that in pastoral work this new theology
is dumb. It is struck with paralysis by the
side of the frightened, the hardened, or peni-
tent sinner, or the dying man and the dying
child. It is dumb in the school. It is dumb
in a man's own chamber. It cannot pray. It is
the pastor, he who ministers to the human soul
in its needs, who is the authority on experience;
and from the aggregate evidence and conclusions
of the pastor, that is, of experience, there lies no
appeal.

Slowly is built up the temple of religion, in
which man meets God. Every age, every
nation, every religion has its contribution to
make; and it is our privilege, as pastors in the
Church of England, to have good grounds
for believing that we also may contribute,
according to our ability, to that supreme work.

God has given to that Church a great mission to a great race and in a great age; and if we are faithful we may do something permanent, however small, in building up His Temple. I know no greater call to Holy Orders than this.

LECTURE VI

ABSTRACT

THE subject of this lecture the pastor's attitude towards his own special flock.

The attractiveness of pastoral work.

The pastor is the representative of the ideal and spiritual sides of life. The natural religious instincts of a congregation.

Their need of idealism.

The need of teaching as to the Atonement; of comfort under the sorrows and stress of life; of inspiration to action; of rebuilding of shattered faith.

To know of these needs in individuals is the best preparation for sermon-writing and other pastoral work.

Early years of the ministry in some respects the most fruitful.

It is said that there is widespread indifference and unbelief.

On analysis this indifference is often a rightful suspension of judgment.

Unbelief also needs analysis. Our need of modesty; of refraining from judging others; and of simplicity.

Final words: the security for the fulfilment of the pledge taken in Holy Orders rests on the continuity of personal identity.

VI

THE PASTOR'S ATTITUDE TOWARDS HIS CONGREGATION

I HAVE now completed my attempt to show what a sphere for varied, thoughtful, progressive activity is offered by the ministry of our Church. It is no *cul-de-sac :* there is room in it for ability and goodness of every kind. Indeed, I can honestly congratulate you on your choice, if you choose Holy Orders as your life's work. From a rather large acquaintance with town clergy in the North, I can confidently say that they are almost universally vigorous, earnest, hopeful, happy. I meet none who wish they had been something else; the *militia est potior* is a sentiment unknown to us. And the reason is plain. Our work is of a kind which to a man of ordinary sympathy and brotherliness and intelligence constantly grows in interest. It places us in natural, unsought, and welcome relations with nearly all the people round us. And this is almost the greatest happiness a man can have. Two young men of similar calibre and character go to live in a town, and one of the two is a curate. Of these two the one cannot at once come, the other cannot help coming, into personal, kindly, happy, and ever-growing relations with all sorts of people. It is this that makes life rich and full, for it gives what human nature needs, the linkage of the part to the whole.

Moreover, this work is indescribably varied. The description of the town parson's day, take what day you will, would be so interesting that any one on reading it would say that of course it was an exceptional, not an average, day. But with all these interesting and important details of work I cannot now deal.[1]

Again, a curate cannot help feeling that he is wanted. There are more doctors and lawyers and schoolmasters than can find

[1] See Father Dolling's *Ten Years in a Portsmouth Slum*, or the Rev. Peter Green in the *Treasury* for January 1903.

patients and clients and pupils.   But no clergyman is struggling with others for his bread,
and no one finds himself superfluous.   Society
would not offer him, as Carlyle says it would
offer others, "a good round sum to go and hang
himself."   If he is kindly, sincerely religious,
unaffected, and industrious, his people do more
than welcome him ; they love and respect him
for his own sake, and for what he represents.
These human relationships, and this sense of
being wanted, sweeten life.   If they lead, as
they should lead as your experience deepens,
to the sympathy of heart with heart in prayer,
and in conversation, and in real friendship,
then life is more than sweet, it is blessed.

I have spoken in successive lectures of a
pastor's essential qualifications ; of his attitude
towards social questions, towards scientific and
philosophic problems, towards the Bible, towards the Church at large, and all the varied
elements that compose his parish ; and now it
remains in this my last lecture to think of his
mental attitude towards his own special flock.
What is he to them ?—a Director ? a Priest ?
a Teacher ? an Example ? a Messenger ? a

Watchman? a Steward of the Lord? an
Awakener of the unconverted? a Shepherd of
the converted? the Channel and Minister of
the Grace of God? Yes! he is all these and
more, if God enables him "to perceive and
know what things he ought to do, and also
gives him grace and power faithfully to fulfil
the same."

He is to them, in these and other ways,
often the sole accredited representative of the
ideal, spiritual, unearthly, eternal side of life.
Think of this. The sole representative! The
church is the one consecrated building in the
parish; consecrated by immemorial tradition
and sentiment, as well as by law. The cross
it uplifts is often the one permanent material
witness to Christ, and the parson the one man
solemnly set apart, perhaps for a lifetime, as
the pastor in things divine of all those souls.
If he is unfaithful, there is no one else to take
his place. His presence excludes others.
This thought should stimulate us to the
utmost, and help to keep us faithful.

Let us look at some of the ideal and
spiritual sides of life, in order to focus more

clearly the nature of pastoral work with our own people : and for the moment we will think chiefly of preaching ; for in church we see our own people collected. Let us think of the congregation, as it gathers for a service.

Why do they come ? What draws them in winter from their comfortable firesides, or in summer from sunny fields and lanes? There is, deep founded in their hearts and souls, a natural religious instinct and ideal. That ideal is the product of centuries of English Christianity ; not of our ancient Church alone, but of Puritan and Nonconforming Church-manship as well. It is the sober fear of a Living God, and trust in His Providence ; it is the love of justice and domestic purity ; in a word, it is that which we define in our Litany as "the true worshipping of God, righteousness and holiness of life." This is the centre and heart of their religion ; and a very noble centre—the light of God Himself in their hearts. Life is often very difficult for them, very stern, very obscure. They do not want light-hearted amateur solutions from young men who do not know life ; but they do

need and value an ideal of righteousness and
holiness; and they do need and desire the
thought of God our Father, of Christ our
Saviour, and the Holy Spirit our Comforter,
the thought of worship, of prayer, of duty, to
be kept before them. We have not in England
the Scotch love of dogmatic precision, nor the
love of the Latin race for "assisting" at a
ceremonial; but we have a truly English
feeling for religion which we must try to
understand, to gratify, and to educate and
strengthen.

What our men and women want is a consecration of Sunday by reverent and real
worship, that supplies a felt hunger in their
hearts. There is a power in public worship
to uplift, to encourage, to assure us of the
reality of the spiritual world, to enable us to
realise the existence of "the mystical body."
It inspires and stimulates as nothing else
does.

Sermons also are enjoyed—" we want to
hear good words on a Sunday," as one of our
congregation said to me. They love to hear
the Bible well read, the prayers really prayed,

the confession said as sins should be confessed, hymns and chants well chosen, well sung. Reverence, reality, truthfulness, warmth—these are the necessities. Nothing but Idealism, idealism in worship, art, and instruction, can stir the souls and warm and comfort and uplift the hearts of those who live all the week in hard, monotonous, exacting, and often anxious work. Never forget how ceaseless the pressure is on them—how far greater it is than anything we have ever borne. You will be surprised at many things when you come to work, but at nothing more than at the value and reality to the working folk of those services that you may now be treating lightly, as if they were a routine, and an interruption, and even a bore.

If you come among them as a true man, with any sympathy, with any real insight into those difficulties of life which try faith and test temper ; any respect and reverence for men and women who are undergoing far harder discipline, far deeper experiences, than yours ; any reasoned hopefulness and confidence in God ; above all, with any spirit of love as to brothers in Christ, "incorporate in the mystical body"—then you will not fail to learn as well as teach, and then you may teach as well as learn.

What are the needs, the desires, of the congregation to whom we shall be called to minister? Put aside for a moment those, if there are any, who feel no need and have no desire, who are satisfied if the service "goes" in the usual way, and the sermon is of the ordinary length, and in familiar phrase, with nothing in it so interesting or real as to excite a suspicion of its orthodoxy. Besides these full-fed and lazy sheep, of whom there *may* be some, there certainly and always are sheep that are hungry; and it is these whom we are bidden to feed. Can we read in their eyes, or imagine, what it is they need?

As we get to know them, we learn that one is saying, "Teach me. I read about Jesus Christ; but it all seems so unreal, to have happened so long ago, so far away. I do not see Him: I love Him, I sometimes think; but I do not understand. Death is drawing near to me, day by day; and life is very perplexing.

Teach me His words, and how I may live in His spirit, and be safe. Help me to understand. How did His coming, His death, affect me? Would not all the world be going on just the same if it had never happened? I am sore perplexed: teach me. How did Christ save me?"

There are times when we can do without answering this question; when we can rest on centuries of Christian experience that He does save us; when we can simply say, with the hymn:—

> He died that we might be forgiven;
>   He died to make us good:
> That we might go at last to Heaven,
>   Saved by His precious blood.

But you will not meet the needs of these hungry sheep till you have the Gospel of the Atonement in your heart of hearts; founded on the Incarnation and the essential Divinity of Christ, and purged from the crudities with which it has been so long associated.

And another says: "Comfort me. This life has brought me strangely little joy. I am surrounded with troubles and bereavements;

life is monotonous and weary, and often sad:
I am getting old, and I see no hope of change.
Heaven seemed nearer when I was a child.
Comfort me. Must this weary life go on un-
relieved till strength fails, and darkness comes
over me, and I sink into the unknown beyond?
Surely Christ came to comfort such as me.
Have you no strengthening word for such as
we are, who toil and sleep and die?"

And to meet these needs we must have
more than a kindly, sympathetic, cheery word
and manner; we need to "comfort them which
are in any trouble, by the comfort wherewith
we ourselves are comforted of God."

Another of a different temperament says:
"Inspire me: lead me into action. Tell me
what to do." I wish there were more of these;
but there are always some; and we must think
of them. There is always, if we can but find
it, the element of heroism in human nature;
and that gift, except where it is very strong, an
exceptional gift of God, is only brought out by
the call to heroism. Such an one says: "I have
taken Christ as my Hero, my Leader: there
is none like Him; I see in Him the Saviour

of the world. I will work for Him; but you must tell me how. I want no arguments—I want to share in noble action. Noble action justifies and verifies my faith." There is a great deal of latent heroism in our race; and I fear our Church is slow to see and utilise it. Here is something for us all to do. Christianity is essentially a heroic religion; and when the heroic side of it is concealed, in order to make it acceptable to the unheroic, it becomes tasteless even to them. For even the unheroic appreciate heroism in others.

And there is yet another type of churchgoer. Whoever else may be absent from church, there is one type always present, often least individualised—the one who would say: "Rebuild my shattered faith. I once thought that the Christian creed was the expression of a real solution of the mystery of this world. I think so no longer. It may be a symbol of a solution: it may be a garment that conceals the truth. But I want more than a symbol or a garment. Have you anything to say on this life of ours and its meaning?" Such an one appeals to us to show that we have got

behind the conventionalities, and have at any
rate begun to fall

> Upon the great world's altar-stairs,
> That slope through darkness up to God.

It is a tremendous appeal; and it comes
from hundreds who are present in our churches,
and from the thousands who are not there.
"You, sir," such an one may be pictured as
saying—"You, sir, are presumed to have
fathomed these things; you have studied
theology. Show us that a Divine Justice is
still ruling the world; find Him in the secret
places of our own hearts; tear away all that
conceals Him in your mediæval phrases, and
show us still in your Church a living and not
a dead God, whom you call on us to worship.
The services of the Church cannot soothe or
inspire or teach us, unless we are shown how
they can be joined in by those who have lost
the old childlike faith. Can you show us how
to read into the old words a greater and truer
meaning than ever?"

Experience will soon bring before your
imagination other types of hearers—those who
are under stress of strong temptation, and who

need to be taught how to seek God's power to keep them from evil. There are those to whom duty is losing its divine, supernatural sanction ; those who are failing to find in the Bible the old stimulus and inspiration it once gave. You must call them up in turn before your thoughts, and think of them in your prayers. To know in this way your congregation and people, as men and women who desire teaching and comfort and inspiration, and the strengthening of faith, is the best preparation for sermons and for all relations with your people. It is to feel that the work is real, that you are dealing with realities, and that you must "draw all your cares and studies this way," in order to make yourself worthier of so great a call.

But I would add, that for many of these duties and relations of which I have spoken the earliest years of a ministry have special advantages, and are sometimes the richest and most fruitful. The higher men rise in the Church, the more do the duties of administration remove them from some of those happy and simple relations with the multitude of young and old in a parish. You enter at once on

your best years. Inexperience is a drawback
in some of your duties; it is none at all in
cultivating human, friendly relations with your
people ; and youth has a charm that age has
lost and cannot regain.

And if these early years of your ministry
are fruitful to others, they are incomparably so
to yourself. There is no epoch so inspiring
in a young man's life as when he first takes
Holy Orders, when he comes to his first
parish to learn how to love and teach and
lead his people to Christ. His daily work
widens his mind and enlarges his heart. It
will be really a simple gospel you will preach,
and it will be the gospel of your life—that
Christ has shown us that God and man are
so united that therefore we are all "partakers of
the divine nature," and must respect ourselves
and all others for the infinite potentialities
of this divine life. This creates a bond of
sympathy, even with strange and perverted
natures in which the divine likeness is blurred.

But you will perhaps be thinking that I am
somewhat highly colouring the desire of a
congregation for teaching, comforting, inspira-

tion, and strengthening of their faith. For do we not hear everywhere of widespread indifference to religion, and of widespread unbelief? Are not these, to a candid mind, plainly the characteristics of our age? Is it wise or fair to ignore these characteristics of those outside our churches when we are thinking of our congregation within them?

We must clear our minds upon this point, or we shall be ourselves repeating the same shallow judgment. *Indifference to what? Unbelief of what?* And *in whom* are the indifference and unbelief we are thinking of? We must focus our glasses, and test generalisations such as these by individualisation. We must not confound indifference to us clergy, or to what we have to say, with indifference to religion and to God; or confuse some people's unbelief in what they have mistakenly come to think is the Christian message with unbelief in the eternal verities. We do the men outside, and still more those inside our churches wrong, if we think of them as universally indifferent to religion. People are often inexpressive, unanalytical. A man may be indifferent to the clergy, but he is not indifferent to religion, as he conceives it. He may suspend his judgment on a good many points to which we professionally attach importance, and we may call that state of mind unbelief. But think how much he has in common with us. We all mean exactly the same thing by a Christian act, temper, and character. The Christian character is as much his ideal as it is ours; and are we sure that he is much farther from it? He is quite sure that religion ought to help a man to be better: that it ought "to do more," as Canon Newbolt has said, "than enable a man to pronounce shibboleth with an ecclesiastical accent." By all that touches this practical religious side of life he is impressible. The enormous sale of religious novels, and other publications, such as Mr. Sheldon's *In His Steps* and similar books, ought to dispel any illusion we may be under as to widespread indifference to religion, or widespread unbelief in Christ as the only possible King of this world. I feel sure that our Lord would not have spoken of "widespread indifference or unbelief" in quite our ordinary tone.

I am not underrating the gravitation towards evil that we must always reckon with
as the counter-influence to the work of the
Spirit of God : there are and ever will be the
temptations of the world and the flesh and
the devil; and there is in our age a terrible
strain, bodily and mental, for some, and an
unendurable monotony of labour for others.
We see the effect of all this in many phenomena : in hysteria ; in spiritualism ; in the rush
for amusements and gambling ; in the passion
for success in competition.   The strain of city
life among the poor is terrible : it is one of
the causes of drink.   " Drink," as one of our
judges said lately, " is the shortest way out of
Manchester."   No one ought to underrate the
illiterate grossness of much of town life.

Our generation of town dwellers perhaps
finds less room and time in heart and life than
did our fathers for the higher interests of
thought, of training of character, of religion.
But these interests are not killed; they are
close to the surface, full of life, ready to be
called out when the hour comes and the
man.

And is indifference to our personal teaching and services to be severely regarded as a sign of spiritual decay?   Let each one of us call up one by one the five or six churches nearest our own, and ask ourselves whether, if it became our fate to be parishioners in that particular parish, we should be enthusiastic.   Would there not be a real fear of our being ranked as indifferent?   Such a reflection may help us to understand how laymen regard us.   Nor is it wonderful, or a reproach to us.   Few men possess the gift of speaking well and interestingly, or even lucidly, on any subject.   The members of the House of Commons are all picked men ; we outnumber them by thirty to one ; but how few of their speeches do we wish to hear or read ? which of them could speak interestingly twice a week for forty years? Yet we are not indifferent to politics.   Do not let us confuse indifference to us with indifference to the eternal world and the things of God.   Do not let us lightly adopt the prevailing cant about "widespread indifference." When you young men begin to preach, not because a sermon must be delivered, but because you have something you *must* say, you will find little that you will call indifference.

And I must say one word to caution you against a similar unthinking charge against the world of "unbelief." It is a most important matter for clergy to understand. The tone of unbelief has greatly changed, and what clergy often say of it is now twenty or even fifty years out of date. Scepticism to-day is serious, not light-hearted ; conscientious, not scoffing ; it is often full of sadness and pain : it is passing here and there into a deeper and stronger but humbler faith, returning to older and simpler lines. It is constantly, as we can all see, associated with a splendid ideal and active life of duty and service and patience, which may well claim our respect for the faith from which it springs. There may be forms and phases of unbelief with which I am not familiar. But I am familiar with what some call unbelief, but which should rightly be called suspension of judgment. This is simply the result of the unconscious acceptance of the axiom of scientific method. That axiom is, in Huxley's words, that "it is our duty to give unqualified assent to no propositions but those the truth of which is so clear and distinct that they cannot be doubted." If this is a sin, then science, and even reason itself, are of their father the devil. But if they are of God, and part of His way of leading the world to a knowledge of Himself, then the attitude of suspension of judgment, of accepting truths as provisional hypotheses, as working bases of conduct, with degrees of assent varying from implicit trust to a balance of probability, is not a sin, but a duty. "Unbelief" is sometimes only an insolent name for a different, and it may well be a juster, proportion of faith. Professor Chase has recently said that "inability to rank all articles of the Creed on the same level is not equivalent to the denial of any." [1] It will be part of your work to assist in this readjustment of the proportion of faith.

I press on you once more the duty of great respect for all men, and great modesty. How few of us clergy—how very, very few—are at all capable, by education, by experience, and

---

[1] "The Supernatural Element in our Lord's Earthly Life," a paper read at Sion College, 21st October 1902. Macmillan and Co.

by natural ability, to enter into the philosophic difficulties that gather round any expression of religion.

There is much else that should give us pause ere we talk of "prevailing unbelief." We may reflect that there is scarcely one of the clergy who is not in the attitude of "suspension of judgment" towards statements which some other clergy think it their duty to reiterate as truths, and deem of great importance. And as a rule we are far less patient with one another under such circumstances than laymen are with us. We may reflect also on the way in which the stubborn, and sometimes bitter, resistance to new light and truth, which clergy have constantly shown, strikes an earnest and simple man outside our ranks.

As I have explained before, it is not the duty of us all to be students of criticism or philosophy, or of more than the elements of theology. It is quite plain, at least to any one who has long examined for Holy Orders, that the majority of clergy are not gifted with qualifications for such studies. They are quite right to renounce them, and to devote themselves to the direct work of highest usefulness, to truly pastoral work, which appeals primarily to qualities of heart and sympathy, and not to those of intellect. But in renouncing such studies a man also finally renounces the right to criticise and condemn students. His own work is a noble one, the offering of an ideal life to all. He has chosen his own path. He must not grudge to others a path on which he does not, and cannot, walk. Our duty is to say with Nicodemus, "Doth the Gospel condemn any man before it hears him?" and run the risk of the retort sure to be once more made, "Art thou also of Galilee?"

There are also phenomena which we must learn to distinguish from unbelief. When we endeavour to explain, in terms of the intellect, our spiritual emotions or impressions, and the motions of our conscience, our explanations will certainly differ, as musicians would differ in attempting to express by music the impressions produced on them by a landscape, or artists in attempting to express their ideals in form and colour. Such explanations as we offer are to be treated not objectively or scientifically, as we treat things in a material world. Differences of expression in such matters are not unbelief. And as all musicians and all artists have more in common with one another than with any less gifted souls, so all spiritual tempers have more in common with one another than with the temper which is not spiritual. And there is much that is truly spiritual in reverent agnosticism.

Humility, therefore, humility, humility. This is essential. Also great simplicity—the teaching of Christ Himself. Recall the words of Erasmus: " I could wish that those frigid subtleties were either completely cut off, or were not the only things the theologians held as certain, and that the Christ pure and simple might be implanted deep within the minds of men." Above all, the presentation of a gospel of a divine Mediator who saves men from sin. Here we rest on an experience which cannot be questioned. Deep in the heart of man is the felt need of a link with God, the Eternal, the Infinite, the Ideal of man ; and the historic Christ is that link, and awakens in each soul, at the moment

that he is fit for it, the divine Life which
Christ came to reveal.

I am speaking still of your attitude towards
your own special congregation, and the diverse
elements there assembled before you.   No
doubt there are differences between town and
country, between South and North, between
West End and East End.   But the resemblances are deeper than any differences ; and
I have aimed at implanting in your mind my
own conviction that below all the perplexing
and bewildering phenomena of our time, at
bottom there is a solid faith, too big, I believe,
and too strong to be forced into the vessels
which were once large enough to contain it.
New bottles are needed for the new wine ;
and the new bottles cannot be made to
order.   We may have to pass through a long
age in which men may feel that conduct is
of great importance, but that the sanction
for conduct is undiscoverable ; in which faith
is essential, and yet the reasons for faith are
inaccessible or incommunicable.   If this is so,
then pastoral care, to prevent the wreck of
lives, to co-ordinate noble instincts into right

action, is more needed than ever. The clergy
of your generation may be called on to help
others to live their lives in the greatest freedom of intellectual thought, and in the strictest
obedience to moral instincts. That will be a
life of faith, and that means an unrelaxed hold
on ideals for man as the child of God.

A few words should be said on the attitude
in particular of a young clergyman towards
laymen, and especially towards those of his
own age and similar education, in general
society. This presents a difficulty which is
acutely felt by some of you. " Is it possible,"
you ask, " to assume the tone and sentiment
of denouncing sin without such forcing of one-
self as to be unnatural and even hypocritical?
On the one hand, any want of sternness may be
felt as condoning sin, and even as encouraging
it; and on the other, until one is more schooled
into the mind and temper of Christ, is it right
to denounce it? Will not our words smack of
officialism, and widen the cleavage between
layman and cleric?"

When I read letters from some of you that
put this difficulty, almost in these words,

before me, it happened that Björnson's story, *The Fisher Maiden*, was lying by me, and I turned to this passage (p. 247): "To my mind," says Odegaard — in speaking of the dangers which attend other professions—" To my mind that calling is most apt to lead us into temptation which induces us to think ourselves righteous because we bring a message from the Righteous One; which deludes us into believing that we have faith because we preach faith to others; or, to speak more plainly, to my mind the priest's calling presents the greatest temptations of all."

The difficulty is a real one : the temptation to pose is real ; and to yield is very damaging. No general answer can, in the nature of things, be given, because it is our own best personalities, and not those of others, that we must express. But some isolated remarks may be useful.

No young man can perhaps fully realise what sin is, because he has not yet seen its consequences. "The spirit of your life is lightness and hope." Yes ; but you know the need of strictness, the awful power of tempta-

tions from the body, which should make one
very merciful and tender in judging others;
and you cannot know the results of sins. You
may have in your memory the words, " Be
sure your sin will find you out." Will you
add to it the yet more searching reading of
the LXX version, " Ye shall know your sins
when the evils overtake you." It is experience
that gives the knowledge and the horror of
sin, and you cannot at once assume the air of
experience.

Then ask yourself what was our Lord's
attitude towards sin and sinners. I see no
trace in Him of what we should describe as
" being shocked." He was as far from this
as from encouraging sin. He denounced no
sins except those of the religious self-deceivers,
the Pharisees. He was indignant with these,
and with these only. Try to picture Him as
He sat at meat with publicans and sinners, or
indeed with Simon the Pharisee. We picture
Him as perfectly natural, and feeling nothing but
sympathetic sorrow for those who were spoil-
ing and losing their best selves, their true life.
We picture Him as unconsciously bringing out

the best side of each man from natural sympathy with Himself. Surely it is possible for a young clergyman in nearly every company so to join in a conversation as to bring out some other and overlooked side; to modify some sweeping and harsh censure of a class or an individual by a remark suggesting a different point of view. We all know people who do this naturally.

But I said "in nearly every company." If we could not trust ourselves in a particular company to be able to say, "Shut up, you brute!" when that might be the only suitable remark, don't let us go into that company. A young man could scarcely imitate Jowett's rebuke, "I think that remark had better not have been made"; still less his well-known treatment of the situation when a guest of distinction at his own table launched on a story that was plainly going to be indelicate: "Let us join the ladies, and finish the conversation in the drawing-room." We must feel strong enough to take our own line anywhere, and not be driven to sheepish silence, where such silence would be a disgrace.

Again, we need not think much about our "influence"—about "doing good." If we can be near to God in ourselves, influence follows. Go rather into society with the wish to get good than to do it. Is it not the very essence of the prig to think himself responsible for putting others right? Above all, be not a prig. Be yourself: but take infinite pains by prayer and humble looking up to God to make yourself better than you are; and then the discipline and experience of pastoral life solves these difficulties for you. Only let us grow in grace.

I have come to the end of my time, and will only say one thing more. When I took Holy Orders at the age of forty-three, a difficulty was placed strongly before me by a scientific friend. I do not doubt you feel it. At the time I was utterly unable to reply. "How," he urged, "can you clergy pledge yourselves as to what you *will* believe? Here is the great workshop of the world's thought humming with business in every department. Criticism, science, philosophy, history, all are working overtime; everything is an open question, and new truth constantly coming to light. How can you say, whatever you believe now, what you will believe ten years hence? "

I felt there was a reply; but I could not express it then. Can you? It is this. Your pledge to believe in Christ or to follow Him is one of a *personal* kind. You know enough of yourself, and enough of Him, to make it quite certain that as long as your identity is maintained you will love and follow and reverence and worship Him. The pledge thus rests on the security of personal identity. You will find more in Christ; you will develop new power in yourself; but it is not possible that anything inharmonious between yourself and your Master can spring up. You know Whom you have believed.

I shall not shrink from saying that such a pledge is like that of marriage; only far more secure. The pledge to love in marriage is given, it might be urged, in entire uncertainty. Who knows how much both may change? But the reply is plain : that the personal identities do not change, but only develop under mutual influence. The instinctive attachment begun in youth ripens, deepens, and matures in age. Your affinity to Christ, your realisation of sonship to God, and of the need of doing His work, does not evaporate or change with a discovery in criticism or science.

You have heard the saying of Confucius, that fishermen use baskets to catch fish; and when they have got the fish, they forget the baskets. You too may, as you grow, forget some baskets, but it will be when you have discovered and rightly value the fish within the baskets.

So once more, with all my heart, I congratulate you on the work you have chosen, and let us pray that God will ever guide and enlighten you in this path of service.

APPENDIX TO LECTURE II

THIS bibliography has been kindly furnished me by Mr. T. R. Marr, M.A., Warden of the Men's House at the University Settlement, Ancoats, Manchester.

A BRIEF BIBLIOGRAPHY ON SOCIAL QUESTIONS

General Studies of Facts as they are, with special reference to Poverty

Poverty: a Study of Town Life, by Seebohm Rowntree. Macmillan, 1901. 10s. 6d. Popular Edition, 1902. 2s. 6d.

Life and Labour of the People in London, by Charles Booth. Macmillan, 1892.

Life in West London, by Arthur Sherwell. Methuen. 2s. 6d.

[The above works are valuable, not only for the facts they contain, but for the accounts given of methods of investigation.]

Problems of Poverty, by John A. Hobson. Methuen. 2s. 6d.

Temperance

The Temperance Problem, by Joseph Rowntree and Arthur Sherwell. Hodder and Stoughton. 7s. 6d. Cheap edition, 6d.

Drunkenness, by Geo. R. Wilson. Swan Sonnenschein. 2s. 6d.

Trade Unionism and Industrial Conditions

History of Trade Unionism, by Beatrice and Sidney Webb. Longmans, 1902.   7s. 6d.

Industrial Democracy, by Beatrice and Sidney Webb.   Longmans, 1902.   12s.

Workers on their Industries, by F. W. Galton.   Swan Sonnenschein.   2s. 6d.

The State and its Children, by Gertrude Tuckwell.   Methuen.   2s. 6d.

Our Industrial Laws, by Mona Wilson.   Duckworth & Co.

Co-operation

The Co-operative Movement, by Beatrice Potter.   Swan Sonnenschein.   2s. 6d.

The Co-operative Movement of To-day, by G. J. Holyoake. Methuen.   2s. 6d.

Labour Co-partnership, by H. D. Lloyd.   Harper and Brothers, 1899.

Housing and Health Problems

The Housing of the Working Classes, by Dr. E. Bowmaker. Methuen.   2s. 6d.

Public Health and Housing, by Dr. Sykes.   P. S. King.   5s.

For local conditions consult reports of Medical Officers of Health.

Charity Organisation, Poor Relief, etc.

Charity Organisation, by C. S. Loch.   Swan Sonnenschein.   2s. 6d.

The Better Administration of the Poor Law, by W. Chance. Swan Sonnenschein.   6s.

The Origin and Growth of the Friendly Society Movement, by the Rev. J. Frome Wilkinson.   1886.

Mutual Thrift, by the Rev. J. Frome Wilkinson.   Methuen, 1891.   2s. 6d.

Recreation, Clubs, and the Use of Leisure Time

Crime and its Causes, by W. Douglas Morrison.   Swan Sonnenschein.   2s. 6d.

Neighbourhood Guilds, by Dr. Stanton Coit.   Swan Sonnenschein.   2s. 6d.

University and Social Settlements, by Will Reason.   Methuen, 1898.   2s. 6d.

Socialism

Socialism in England, by Sidney Webb.   Swan Sonnenschein. 2s. 6d.

" Merrie England " and " Britain for the British," by Robert Blatchford.   *Clarion* Office, 72 Fleet Street, E.C. 3d. each.

The tracts issued by the Fabian Society (3 Clement's Inn, Fleet Street, E.C.) will be found of value.   Over 100 have been published, each of them dealing with some social question.   Most of them are sold at one penny. A set costs about 2s. 6d.   The tract entitled " What to Read " gives a list of books of great value to Social Reformers.   Price 6d.

Books of Reference Published Annually

The Reformer's Year Book.   London : *Clarion* Office.

The Financial Reform Almanack.   Liverpool :   Financial Reform Association.

The Municipal Year Book.   London : Lloyds.

SCIENCE AND THEOLOGY

OR

An Essay on the Influence
of Scientific Training on the
Reception of Religious Truth

INTRODUCTION

I ASSUME that we may define religious truth
as the application of all that may be known
to elucidate the relation of man to God.
Religious truth is not of a different quality
from other truth; but it is truth consecrated to
a particular purpose. Every one is conscious of
a certain change in the attitude of the human
mind towards religious truth resulting from
the extraordinary development and fresh ap-
plications of the methods of inductive science
during the last century. People may regard
this change as likely to be permanent or
temporary, as favourable or unfavourable to
religion; but the fact of the change is patent.
Also it is practically certain that what is known
as scientific training will become more general
and more complete and thorough. The effect
of the change, moreover, is one which reaches
all classes, because it operates indirectly as

well as directly. We have therefore to consider not only the effect on the student himself
of his scientific training, but also the effect of
the student class, so influenced, on those classes
which at present get no direct scientific training.
In this way, by indirect influence, the effect of
scientific training filters down till it permeates
all classes. Moreover, the effects are cumulative and progressive. The influence therefore
of such training to-day is not the same as it
was thirty years ago, nor even as it was still
more recently. The effect cannot therefore
be summarised as being this or that. It is a
highly complex and varying influence.

As the influence filters down slowly through
the various degrees of education, we see to-day
reproduced, in the lowest class which it has
reached, almost the same arguments and difficulties that were heard thirty years ago in a
higher class. I listened lately to a secularist
orator declaiming in a town square exactly
what would have been said a generation ago
by any educated man of that way of thinking :
but the difficulties of to-day among men of
education are of a different order.

SECTION I

THE UNSETTLING BUT TEMPORARY EFFECTS OF SCIENTIFIC TRAINING

It will be convenient to consider first those effects which we may reasonably regard as temporary, and belonging to a period of transition.

It is perhaps scarcely worth while here to reproduce in any detail the crudeness of the difficulties to which I have referred above. They turn, as one would expect, almost wholly on the incompatibility of the *results* of physical science with the verbal inspiration and literal interpretation of Scripture. They may therefore perhaps be thought not strictly germane to my subject, which is limited to the effects of scientific *training*. But it is important to us all to know that in a certain stratum of

uneducated society these difficulties are still very
real, as the indirect results of scientific training.
The points commonly insisted on are the
impossibility of a sudden creation, the obvious
difficulties of the Mosaic narratives, and the
moral difficulties of the Old Testament.

But sometimes they reach a far higher level;
and much thought and knowledge and sympathy
are required to meet them. I listened some
few years ago to one such lecturer who was
refuting, and refuting very well, the old form
of the Paleyan argument from design. "You
talk," he was, in substance, saying of his
imaginary antagonist, "you talk of the wonderful adaptations in the world. You say that
the world is so exquisitely suited to its
inhabitants, and its inhabitants to the world,
that the design of a great Artificer is manifest.
Of course the world is exquisitely suited to its
inhabitants, or it would not be inhabited by
them. There spring up in the ocean creatures
that can live in the ocean; on dry land, things
that can live on dry land; in deserts, plants
that can live in deserts; in swamps, those that
can live in swamps. If a tree or an animal

were not adapted in all respects to its surroundings it would die. There is no more
design in the eye of a hawk than in the curve
or slope of a sea beach, so admirably adapted
to resist the waves. The one is the result of
the unconscious, purposeless action of the
waves; the other the result of the unconscious
struggle for existence and the survival of the
fittest." And he went on to speak of Design.
" How can mind, will, interfere with matter and
act on it? The action on physical matter must
be physical, material. The world is one vast
mechanical system. Everything is determined
by what preceded it. There is no room for
design in a world of which the supreme characteristic is universal physical law and physical
sequence. It is only a question of complexity
of causation; our thoughts are the results of
motions of the molecules of the brain; and if
one knew all antecedents, and if our means of
calculation were adequate, it would be possible
to predict all consequences."

The effect of scientific training, it will be
seen, on this type of mind is to present to it an
alternative between natural evolution by the

constant action of invariable and unconscious
forces, and supernatural creation with design
determining each detail as the need arises.
" Choose," he said in fact, " between Nature
acting by natural invariable laws which science
unerringly reveals, and God acting arbitrarily
and supernaturally of whom the theologians
and the priests speak.   Choose," he repeated,
" between these two.   For there is no third
alternative."   And all this was not easy for
his hearers to see through or to answer.

I am not now going to deal with the fallacy
of the alternative, and the exclusion of the
third choice, of God acting in the physical
realm by invariable laws, some of which science
is revealing ; nor with the fallacy of the opposition of natural and supernatural, an antithesis
as fatal to science as it is to theology.   With
the methods of dealing with men in this condition I am not now concerned.   But it is
obvious that to assume that this alternative
exhausts the possibilities is a barrier to the
reception of religious truth ; and it is a very
necessary part of the training of the Christian
apologist of to-day that he should be enabled

to meet with confidence such a man on his own ground. The belief that men are shut up to this alternative is beyond question an effect on a certain class of mind of scientific training, and it is very unfavourable to the reception of religious truth, since it excludes all thought of God, of freedom of the will, and therefore of morality. We shall see later how best to deal with these difficulties.

I have purposely taken the instance of a man of far more than average ability, who faced his thoughts to the best of his power, who clearly expressed, and boldly avowed them. There are very many more who share these impressions, but are unable to formulate them. On them the result is a certain vague unexpressed materialism. This materialism shows itself in a common attitude towards education and legislation. It is impossible to mistake a prevailing feeling about education. It is that technical education is the really nation-forming influence, reinforced by other branches of useful knowledge ; but that there is a prejudice still surviving among less advanced and old-fashioned minds, that not only ethical advice and rules, but actually speculative and dogmatic truths should be taught in schools; and for the sake of peace this is conceded for the present till the prejudice dies out. This feeling, so far as it prevails, is in considerable measure one of the results of scientific training; and it is a really dangerous result. For if it reached a point at which a general abandonment of old principles in education became necessary, experience seems to show that national disintegration and mutual distrust must after a time set in.

A similar effect of scientific training is to weaken the religious faculties by mere disuse. In an essay, "On Teaching Natural Science in Schools," which I wrote as long ago as 1867 I find these words, and I cannot say the same thing better: "The vague impression that reverence, faith, belief in the unseen and the spiritual, and in truths derived from individual consciousness, are diminished, as superstitions are diminished, by the school of science, must not be met by an offhand denial that there is any foundation for it; for constant dealing with nature and the exercise of the intellect alone, as contrasted with humanity and the exercise of the moral feelings, unquestionably tend to exclude men from the highest thoughts. . . . The constant study of one kind of evidence raises a secret disinclination, and real inaptitude for the time being, to accept evidence of a different kind, and induces men openly or tacitly to depreciate and distrust it. They are continually tempted to consider the finer mental and religious sensibilities as useless, and as if they proved nothing. They are facts, of course, but verge on fancies; and men so trained have acquired a distaste for this kind of reflection, and something of contempt for its value in others. They seem to have raised a wall between themselves and certain truths; to have dazzled their eyes by a study of the glaring truths of external nature, and to be for the time incapable of discerning the dimmer but nobler truths of the Soul and its relations."[1]

It is not for a moment to be thought that the training in the physical sciences has in it anything in itself demoralising; it is simply that the imaginative and the introspective,

[1] *Essays on a Liberal Education.* Macmillan.

Q

emotional, and religious faculties are liable to
be dwarfed by disuse.

Another result of training in scientific
methods is still very common. It is to make
men profoundly dissatisfied with the methods
and principles of much of the religious teaching
that has been given them. They have become,
through their scientific training, aware of the
difficulty of ascertaining truth, of the many
sources of error, of the imperfection of our
faculties, senses, and judgment; they have
learned that many theories, confidently held
at one time and taught as facts, have been
abandoned, and that we are compelled to
hold many opinions as merely provisional, as
useful colligations of facts, but as only imperfectly representing those facts. And to minds
so trained there comes the conviction that
much of what was taught them in connection
with religion was taught without due regard
for accuracy and truthfulness. And this discovery creates a strong prejudice against all
that was so taught, and against all its teachers.
I have personally known distinguished men of
science who have spoken to me of their early

religious teaching (which was not exceptionally bad) as a crime committed against them—a crime which they could never forgive, and of which they could never obliterate the effects. The Bible was "spoiled for them for ever." There is no stronger reason for the most scrupulously truthful religious teaching than this terrible, and very common, reaction in the minds of those who have been ill taught. The way to avoid and minimise this most serious effect of scientific training on the reception of religious thought is so to teach religion in every home, and every school, from the infant school to the university, that men and women shall have as little as possible to unlearn ; or, in a word, to prepare religious thought for scientific training by making the religious teaching truthful, and not inconsistent with scientific methods and results.

Closely connected with this is the effect of scientific training on the mind of a man who is too deeply religious by temperament and by early associations to be able to throw off with resentment the misleading teachings of early years, but who continues to feel a life-long struggle between the intellect on the one hand and what he feels as a sort of conscience or immovable prejudice on the other. The results of this struggle are often very sad. In some minds the conviction arises that religious teaching is irreconcilable with truth of fact, and that we must make up our minds to this antagonism. Men may choose, and they themselves have chosen, and there is at their age no going back. Of course such a conviction gives a great sense of weakness and of insecurity in all the religious beliefs which are retained. It induces an exaggeration of the dogmatic character of religious belief; because, as is well known, men make up for the want of certainty by extreme precision of statement; their minds turn away from fundamental truths to matters which only touch them superficially. This makes some men very unhappy. They feel in a false position; they dare not say to any clergyman, scarcely to any layman, what they think. The effect, direct or indirect, of sound scientific training in such cases as these is thus very unsettling; and such men can get no help from their friends, who either know nothing of

their difficulties, or who, like themselves, reso-
lutely keep them under lock and key. It is
plain that on them the indirect effect of scientific training is distinctly unfavourable to their
reception of religious truth.

The result on the most thoughtful members
of the class I am speaking of, men who, possessing a strong religious temperament, have come
under the influence of scientific method, is that
they shift the basis of their faith. They find,
in other words, that their faith does not really
rest where they supposed it did. To this also
I shall recur later.

To sum up. Scientific training accentu-
ates Biblical difficulties; and demands, if faith
is to be preserved, more thought on first principles of Biblical interpretation than is often
given; it accounts for the strong materialistic
bias at present felt in education; it weakens the
religious faculties by leading to their disuse;
it provokes resentment in some minds against
untruthful religious teaching, and in others
leads to a still more emphatic dogmatism of
despair. Nevertheless in the more thoughtful
minds even at present scientific training is

leading to the establishment of faith on firm foundations other than those which had been undermined.

Such seem to me to be the most obvious and general effects of scientific training upon the reception of religious thought. The main thing to notice in them is that they are distinctly temporary, and belong to a time of transition. All these effects are passing away; some have almost completely passed away from certain levels of education.

SECTION II

I PASS on now to some of the more obvious
changes which seem likely to be permanent.

Science has, of course, infinitely widened our
conception of the universe as to its extent in
space, its duration in time, and as to the incon-
ceivable complexity of what is spoken of as
matter and ether. By familiarising us with
infinities of space and time it has also rendered
impossible to the scientific mind certain primi-
tive and anthropomorphic conceptions of
God which haunt popular religious literature.
Science has completely altered men's conceptions of creation. Science tells us not of
creation but of development. We have to
interpret creation in the light of evolution;

and this has strained and stretched the old religious philosophy. Again, science has utterly indisposed men to rely on authority. All scientific investigation rests on an appeal to the facts themselves. It has become impossible to any one who has acquired the scientific standard of knowledge to rest content with any assertion without knowing on what facts it is based, and feeling that such facts and assertions are always open to re-examination. The law of gravitation is only accepted because any one may call it in question. Any doctrine of the inspiration of Scripture can only be accepted by scientific minds on the same ground.

The scientific habit of mind compels a man to think what is implied in his creed and his words. The one thing that such a man hates is " muddle "—a confused state of mind, that does not know on what its opinions rest, or whether they rest on anything. A man who has been really influenced by scientific training demands, so far as his abilities go, some degree of precision ; he demands accuracy and lucidity. We may be sure that this is a permanent result of the extension of scientific training. It will be necessary for religious thought and method to be more orderly, more lucid, more cogent, in the future, than it has been in the past.

Again, a further result has been, or surely will be, to raise the standard of knowledge in all matters bearing on religion. Science explores with such minute care into every detail, as a glance at the monographs of any scientific society will show, that it makes men expect the same sort of accuracy and exhaustive care in all those fields which border on religion, such as interpretation, scholarship, antiquarianism, history; and finally in the statements of belief and of duty, in the philosophy of religion, and in the morality it inculcates. Scientific training disposes people to resent all that is slipshod, wordy, inaccurate. This also we may be sure is a permanent effect.

Another result of scientific training has been to raise a barrier more impassable than ever between what we know as the regions of mind and matter. Both regions are but very imperfectly known to us, and their relation to one another is still less known; but closely as they are related, it is becoming more, and not less, impossible to bridge even in thought the interval between them. On the one hand, it is increasingly obvious every day how intimately connected are body and mind ; we know how a slight lesion of the brain affects all the intellectual faculties of a man, and how a little morphia may subvert even his character. There are a thousand illustrations of this. Again, all the latest speculations as to the relations of matter and ether seem to point to matter as a mere motion of ether. But, on the other hand, however close the connection, it is impossible to bridge the interval between mechanism and self-consciousness. Not a single step has been taken or imagined in this direction. We can imagine mechanism of unlimited complexity, like Professor Osborne Reynolds' ether atoms (Rede Lecture, 1902) ; but when all is done we are plainly not one whit nearer the solution of the problem how this mechanism thinks ; how it becomes self-conscious. It is an instrument, an organ, a mechanism, and the more we know about it the wider is the gap that separates the mechanism from the mind that uses it. This is another permanent effect of scientific training. One sees at present semi-scientific people who do not feel this gap, and are dazzled by the little knowledge they possess; but the effect of thorough scientific training is unmistakable. It reveals the permanent chasm between the material and the spiritual.

I am tracing the permanent effects of scientific training on men's reception of religious truth; and one among these, closely connected with what has been just said, is the increased sense of mystery in the universe, and especially of the mystery in man. This has always characterised the true men of science, and the wider and sounder scientific training becomes, the more general is also this sense of mystery. The popular mind is inclined to think that, because we know something about stars and the earth and plants, practically all is known. But to an ever wider circle of scientific people it is not our knowledge but our ignorance that is so surprising. "We know in part and we prophesy in part." And therefore one may possess his soul in patience when listening to materialistic dogmatisers who seem to know everything. They are only for the time. That which is permanent is modesty, awe, reverence for the mystery of things.

A further point is that a real acquaintance with any branch of science compels one to see that religion lies in a wholly different and still more important sphere. One learns how to combine a very high estimate of the dignity and utility of science with an acknowledgment of its insufficiency, nay, its inappropriateness, as a guide to life. It is a mere instrument, a very important instrument, in life, but no more. It is not in science that our true life consists. Provided some one knows how to make a pump or a telegraph, and some one knows what nebulæ are made of, and the properties of argon, this is all we want. It is not of importance to us as human beings that we should all have an independent knowledge of scientific results. We can leave them to specialists. But religion concerns us all; for it supplies nothing less than the inner motive to personal duty and to life. Science does not touch directly the springs of conduct or of ethics, though it supplies much information as to consequences. In fact the more scientific we become, the more clearly do we learn that our scientific faculty, our intelligence, is not ourselves. How easily we lay it aside like a tool! How indifferent to it we are! But our affections, our will, our conscience, the religious faculty, this is central. This we cannot lay aside; this is our very selves. One, therefore, of the permanent influences of scientific training upon men is to teach them how small a part the results of science play in the formation of character of man. Scientific method is an instrument in the training of his faculties for advancing the utilities of life, for widening his knowledge and imagination, but not more.

The natural further consequence already manifest, and likely to be permanent, is that scientific training is affecting the methods of investigation into the realm of religion, and translating them into a higher region, a region of the interaction of the mind and will of man with that of God, the supreme Mind. The nobler, therefore, and wider the range of science becomes, so much the more lofty and ethereal does the region of religion necessarily become. It is a region of mystery; but the mystery does not oppress us, because it is a mystery arising from the limitation of our faculties, and from the nature of our past developments. Hence it would seem to be a permanent result of scientific training that while a man is made more critical and *exigeant* in examining the grounds of his religious faith, yet he is not thereby rendered indisposed to recognise a region in which scientific proof is inapplicable, and in which intuition, *i.e.* faith more or less verified and approved by reason, is supreme. The conviction grows that there exists a reality corresponding to our moral ideals, a conviction just as strong, and just as incapable of proof, as that there exists a reality in matter corresponding to our sensations. That this will be a permanent conviction, at any rate among Western minds, seems probable. The evidence, historical and philosophical, is accumulating in favour of such natural religion.

But, at the same time, a mind, affected by scientific training, applying itself seriously to religion, almost inevitably demands simplicity, and general principles, even amid mystery. It cannot be denied that the scientific mind is rendered fearless, and therefore averse to the refusal to investigate ultimate principles, averse to anything like a timid economy of truth. Hence it would seem to be a permanent effect of scientific training on the reception of religious thought to dispose the mind not to destroy or to dissolve but to simplify; to place truths in clear order and perspective; the dominant and universal truths before others which are derivative and partial; those which are true for all and for all equally before those which specially attract and affect individual minds. Scientific training thus tends also to prevent the disintegration of theology by excessive minuteness.

SECTION III

THE PROBABLE PERMANENT EFFECTS OF SCIENTIFIC TRAINING ON THEOLOGICAL METHODS

STILL more important is the revolution that scientific training is making in theological methods; in presenting the foundations of our belief.

Scientific training will not permit the question to be left in abeyance, as if the decision was unimportant, on what foundation, in the last resort, does our belief in God, and in human responsibility, rest. Does it rest ultimately on the historical evidence for statements contained in the Bible, or on authoritative declarations made by the Church? Does it therefore share in all the weaknesses attaching to such authority, and to the uncertain interpretations of poetry, metaphor, narrative,

240

and the abstract terms of thought used in other languages? Is theology, in a word, an uncertain deduction from precarious and shifting postulates? That it is this in the minds of many persons is certain, who regard it therefore as scientifically worthless, even if practically useful.

Now the most permanent, and perhaps the most important, effect of scientific training is to compel the ultimate adoption in theology of some scientific method of investigation, and to force us to find some firm ground in experience, and in the nature of things, for those beliefs which have been common to the whole human race, and form the foundation of religion. The effect is, in a word, to compel the treatment of theology as a science; and, so far as the method is applicable, as an inductive science. None of us can as yet see all that is implied in this. But this at any rate can be seen: that the effect is to compel us to assume the reality of the phenomena with which religious experience is concerned, and to make them the foundation of faith. The prevalence of scientific method demands serious attention to

R

the science of theology, as one dealing with facts of the highest importance; and submits to verification every stage of the inductions of that science. The ultimate result is to include religion in the realm of universal law.

The consideration of this point of view, even if unfamiliar to us, will help us to understand the mind of the thoughtful layman whose whole education and habit of view are inductive. His religion is a very real thing indeed; but it is based in reality on personal experience, on conscience, on his intuitive knowledge of God. And much of our teaching seems to him to have a wholly different origin. What we say hangs loosely on him, like clothes. It is not a part of himself; he does not wish to throw it off; it would make him feel naked; and he could not make it over again for himself. But for all that it is not really part of himself, it is not clearly co-ordinated with other knowledge. It is an extra, an overcoat, a *superstitio*.

The effect of scientific training is always to promote a search for continuity. Whether it be the contrast between matter and force, solid and liquid and gaseous, animal and vegetable, natural and supernatural, human and divine, the scientific mind searches for transitional forms and conditions.   Hence it is inevitable that a change in the view of revelation will take place.   It will lose something of its apparent discontinuity, and come to be regarded as an influence of the Divine Spirit on the Human Mind, discernible in many forms, seen in operation "at sundry times and in divers manners."   It will be seen that Revelation is part of the actual present organic process of things ; that behind all the facts of history and observation some Purpose is discernible, and that there exists the actual working of an invisible God on the minds of men.   We shall not, therefore, repeat the mistake made by a certain school of naturalists. Some of them seem to have inferred that because there are normal influences at work tending slowly to modify varieties, therefore the appearance of species *per saltum* is incredible.   We shall not infer that because the influence of the Holy Spirit is felt in its degree on all, therefore the doctrine of the

Incarnate Word is incredible. It is all the more assured thereby, and all the more intelligible.

Another great and permanent influence of scientific training is, that it compels us to regard theology as progressive. That morality is progressive we now recognise; and the discovery has made the Old Testament intelligible. But it is a less familiar thought that theology is not a closed science. Of course the mass of what has to be said in a science so old, so world-wide, will be old; but it is like a coral reef: there is always a living and fresh fringe and surface to it. Theology always seems new and living when we ourselves regard it as in direct relation with present facts. What comes with unexpected force is the conviction that in some truth, expressed imperfectly in some familiar dogmatic form, we have the key that fits the lock of the problem of to-day.

How much this association of the thought of progressiveness with theology will affect us it is impossible to say. It appears to me that it will infuse into its study quite a new life. We can tolerate any degree of incompleteness, social, ethical, scientific, theological, provided we recognise the present condition as the pathway, and the only pathway, to something better. But we cannot tolerate imperfection posing as perfection. The thought of progressiveness makes theology alive. It justifies her claim to be the queen of the sciences. Progress cannot be limited to a few classes of study, it must include the highest of all. We may put it down as one of the permanent effects of scientific training that the mind becomes expectant of progress; that is, of more discrimination and selection, and of more reasoned and sounder and wider inductions than those which have passed current as the theology of the past.

This statement as to progressiveness in theology will be perhaps admitted in general, and then denied in any specific instance. But we shall, in fact, learn tolerance through science. We have much to learn, for there is an immense prejudice in favour of regarding theology as unprogressive. And yet how atheistic is the thought of unprogressiveness, when it is once understood. "If the Comforter," said Bishop Thirlwall, "is really to guide men into all truth, then His later lessons may well transcend His earlier." Crude and preliminary generalisations in theology must be superseded by later and juster generalisations, as in every other department of human thought.

I dwell on this progressiveness for many reasons; chiefly because of the extreme reluctance that will be felt to accept the statement that theology, at any time, cannot be more than a summary of the best thought on ultimate problems of man's nature. The reluctance will be extreme to admit a principle which may seem to involve the shaking of the very foundations of religious certitude. For there will be many who feel that all experience is in favour of the practical advantage of certitude. It will be urged that it is in the certitude of the Mohammedan's faith, or of the Romanist's,—in the unalterability of their faith, the superiority to all examination,—that the strength of such faith lies. It is so. Certitude in presence of ignorance makes devotees—but certitude in presence of knowledge makes sceptics; certitude under some conditions makes for strength, but under other conditions it makes for paralysis.

Another consequence of the scientific spirit, obvious indeed, but worth mentioning, is that our assent to some theological dogmas will be more confident than our assent to others. It is a simple matter of observation that the fact is so. We are, as every one will admit, tending towards the holding of a few truths which we trust to more entirely, and towards the holding with a less tenacious grasp other opinions. Illustrations of the fact will occur at once to every one. But the full significance of this fact and its hopefulness may not at once be seen. It was, I believe, a saying of Fichte, that "science converts faith into insight." I take this to mean that the scientific habit of mind, which reasons inductively, when applied, as it must be, to the subjects of human life and ethics, transforms the unanalytic trust in a providential ordering of the world, which we call faith, into a reasoned and profound insight into the laws of God. It means that under the influence of scientific method, faith grows into a reasoned perception of the essential and important truths of life and thought, and leads to the expression of these truths as reasoned certainties. And

it is certain that this will tend to simplification
of dogma and differentiation of certitude.

In this simplification of theology, a transformation which is being slowly effected before
our eyes, lies, I believe, a great hope for the
future of our Church and its theology.   I know
that at this point we come to the parting of
the ways.   At this point *Samios diducit littera
ramos*.

To some temperaments it will seem that the
present fluid state of religious thought calls for
the more explicit, the more unhesitating, and
the more all-embracing dogmatic teaching.   It
will give, as they say, backbone to our teaching.
There is something in what they say.   That
method will get hold of and guide some.   But I
believe that among our people, the proportion
that can be so got hold of and guided is ever
growing smaller, and that it is not in that direction that truth or expediency lies.   The fluid
state of religious thought is no doubt responsible for the fact that religious principles play so
small a part in the great politics of the world, or
of a nation, or of the smaller politics of the home.
But this in its turn arises from the fact that the

confidence in the truths of religion felt by the average man of the world is extremely weak. But if the great moral laws of God, which sum up theology as it affects conduct, should come to be held with the conviction and certitude that follow great inductions perpetually verified, how different may be the influence of religious principles on a nation! It may come by this process to be really felt that morality is of the nature of things, as much as inertia or gravitation. The tendency of scientific thought would seem to be therefore to concentrate certitude on a few plain and central truths, in theology and ethics as in science, and to permit the acceptance of much as provisional hypothesis which up to this time it has been thought unfaithful to question. We may hope for the advantages of certitude without its corresponding evils.

If this prospect of differentiation of certitude seems to any one alarming and unsettling, I would ask him to reflect whether this is wholly unlike our Lord's own method. He placed Himself before His disciples, and they drew their own inferences. He did not hurry them ;

and He did not coerce them. Theology as He laid the foundation of it was a gradual induction from observation, and a progressive interpretation of experience. We cannot but admit that Christian theology, as we know it, took its origin in the interpretation of Christ by a Church in which His Spirit was ever present to lead them towards truth, rather than in dogmatic words from Himself so explicit and final as to preclude all fresh light of revelation. In this sense it may be said that it is not the historic, so much as the living and present Christ, who is the Christ of theology. The historicity of the historic Christ is not impugned, but is confirmed, by this way of regarding the origin of Christian theology.

The harmony between the scientific and the religious mind, which must be the final result of the worthy study of science and religion, will be found in the widest acceptance of the limitation of our faculties, an acceptance alike unwelcome to the student of either science alone or of theology alone. We find ourselves in a world of physical law in which we find it impossible to believe in the disturbing influence of any outside immaterial cause which we may invoke; and we also find ourselves as spiritual beings closely connected with, but apart from matter and controlling it; and we have a first-hand conviction, which we cannot ignore, that our minds and spirits are related to something outside ourselves, and that we are members of a spiritual world, and under its moral laws. We will be modest enough not to deny either material or spiritual world, or to regard either as excluding the other, though we cannot see them in relation to one another. We will not consent to the negations of either science or religion, while we accept their affirmations. Spiritual personality remains, and is a witness to the existence of a world other than the physical. We will recall Matthew Arnold's line

Men must begin, know this, where Nature ends.

SECTION IV

THERE is another probable result of scientific training which is so different from those which I have hitherto spoken of that it requires a separate section.

The scientific training of the laity inevitably involves on the part of theologians a very resolute, prolonged, and impartial examination into the first principles of our religion. This will require not years but centuries. For the advance of the inductive method is in the same relation to Christian thought and doctrine of to-day that the Greek philosophy was when first it was brought into close contact with Christian thought. It is an influence that compels the most exhaustive examination of first principles. In those early centuries the Christian school of Alexandria had to hold its own in open debate against the combination of Greek philosophy and Oriental mysticism; and it is never to be forgotten that out of that fierce discussion sprang the strongest, wisest, and most durable theology the world has yet seen. It led to the Nicene Creed. The extreme freedom of discussion of Christendom of to-day can best be paralleled in the discussions of that age. The Christianity of to-day is already brought into contact with two additional solvents, the inductive philosophy, and the claims of natural religion as witnessed by the ancient Oriental religions, for the first time made known to the West during the last century; and Christianity may yet have to encounter more powerful solvents than these.

And the parallel with the Alexandrian age is closer than this. There was then, as there is now, the apparent antagonism between the two conceptions of God, the indwelling and the transcendent. They are not, indeed, mutually

exclusive : nevertheless it is substantially true
that the theology of the Church, so far as it
is popularly apprehended, is believed to rest
on the latter conception ; and under the influence now of science, as then of philosophy, the
intellectual world can accept only the former.
One great and permanent effect of scientific
training is thus a reversion to the Greek or
Eastern or Athanasian type of theology, and
the re-interpretation of the language of our
formularies in that sense. The religious
philosophy of a religious man of science is
therefore identical in some essential points
with the old Greek orthodox theology. That
theology remains orthodox. It has never
been superseded ; it has only been forgotten.
There is nothing to prevent our recurring to
that orthodox or Johannine simplicity. " This
Word, Who was from the beginning, Who
appeared as new, and yet was proved to be
old, and is engendered always young in the
hearts of Saints, He I say was eternal." So
we read in the Epistle to Diognetus. The
central doctrines of Clement and Athanasius,
if I understand them right, are not incom-

patible with the philosophic spirit that is the result of inductive science. Science can contemplate the doctrine of an Eternal Word, the Teacher and Perfecter of men; and can accept the doctrine of salvation as a renewal of our souls in holiness, and the recovery of the image of God by a true spiritual acquaintance with Him.

The whole conception of Evolution leads to the universal immanence of God. This is and must be the religion of the Evolutionist. I do not of course say that this removes all difficulty; but it is one of the effects of scientific training on the reception of religious truth, that the only theory of God possible to the Evolutionist is that of the indwelling God. The difficulty lies here. Evolution de-anthropomorphises God, and therefore comes perilously near de-personalising Him. Sooner or later we come to this issue. Sooner or later science seems to divest the God of the Evolutionist of everything we can love, and of every definable or imaginable relation to the individual soul. Reason is cogent, inexorable, even when faith remains. God seems lost in the dim infinity of law which science has revealed. Is not then this God of the Evolutionist identical with the God of the Pantheist?

Men stand on the brink of this thought, and shudder at it, as they dip their feet in its chilling stream. But cross it they must; cross it the Church must; on the other side is a faith which has found as yet no exponent.

This is, I suspect, the problem which will tax the next age. The rest of what I have to say will consist of a few suggestions as to our attitude towards it, and its possible developments.

We must acquiesce in a totally imperfect solution. Scientific training has indeed done little for us unless it has taught us that we are as yet almost infinitely remote from complete knowledge. Verily "we know in part," and we shall do well to "prophesy in part." If indeed, as the theistic theory of evolution declares, Nature is the inchoate self-expression of God, we must be still in very early stages of that expression. God must transcend Nature and pervade it, as the mind and will of man transcends his body and pervades it, and that in a far higher degree. No cell of a human body, no microbe in its tissues, can interpret the personality of the whole; and we men simply cannot grasp the Personality of God, and His Love and Fatherhood, when we think of all Nature as the expression of His living and acting Will.

Nevertheless, since reason and righteousness are in man, there must be a rational and righteous reality, evolving Himself in us; and since love is the best in us, there must be love in God. The loving Father must be there; though our poor undeveloped minds cannot simultaneously combine His loving fatherhood with His immanence, and with the uniform working of His laws of nature. I know that this is the problem of philosophy; the passage from the individual and subjective to the universal and objective. It may be impossible to demonstrate the possibility of the passage; but without it there is no knowledge possible to us, and no rationality anywhere.

There is yet another thought for which I should wish to find expression.

Scientific training is not confined to the

study of physical and historical science; it includes the scientific study of ethics. It would be a worthy subject for examination, what is the effect of a systematic study of ethics on the reception of religious truth. I am not qualified to make that examination. But so far as I can trace in my own mind the influence of such studies, elementary as mine have been, it is to give a greater confidence in the objectivity of the moral ideal, by which I mean the best that we are able to conceive. Instead of this presenting itself to us as a mere ideal aim, it tends to come before us as a reality in which our personalities are somehow bound up. The various theories of ethics all seem to require something outside men; some objectivity which embraces them all. There is something which cannot be explained by utilitarianism, or hedonism, or intuition, or their combination. There must be something behind. Now if this is so in any degree it makes the moral ideal much more than an ideal; it assures us that what we call an ideal is really a power working in and for us all. And there is no such source of sustained energy as this belief.

If, indeed, scientific training is found to have
this effect it is a true ally of religion.   And it
is so primarily because it helps us to explain
the lowest by the Highest, to see Nature as
destined to find its explanation and meaning
in that supreme moral reality of which we
have become convinced, and not to see Nature
as the inexplicable development of intricate
mechanical laws.   I say " Nature as destined
to find," for it is impossible in the midst of the
vast æons of evolutionary progress to anticipate the finding.   But this conviction of
evolution, combined with the conviction of a
moral ideal, gives us an assurance of our faith.
It appears to me, but I know that here I am
travelling outside both the range of my proper
subject and my special studies, that the scientific
study of ethics will find a solid basis for that
characteristic of all religions that the individual
feels himself bound to some wider community,
whether family or nation or race, personified
in some Being whom to know and to serve is
man's natural duty.   At our present stage
such personification is regarded by philosophers
as an idealisation ; it will perhaps eventually

be regarded in the opposite light, that the reality of that Person is the cause of our feeling so bound to Him. The early religions may then eventually be seen to have had indeed the limitations of tribalism and national-ism, but to have been the anticipations of a universal and world-wide kingdom of God.

I can cordially adopt the final words of the late Professor Henry Sidgwick in his work on the *Methods of Ethics* :—

" The whole system of our beliefs as to the intrinsic reasonableness of conduct must fall without a hypothesis, unverifiable by experi-ence, reconciling the individual with the Universal Reason ; without a belief, in some form or other, that the moral order, which we see imperfectly realised in this actual world, is yet actually perfect. If we reject this belief, we may perhaps still find in the non-moral universe an adequate object for the Speculative Reason, capable of being in some sense ulti-mately understood. But the Cosmos of Duty is thus really reduced to a Chaos : and the prolonged effort of the human intellect to frame a perfect ideal of rational conduct is seen to have been foredoomed to inevitable failure." [1]

I venture on these general anticipations because scientific method always seems to lead towards general laws and comprehensive views. And if scientific method is profoundly to affect religious thought, it would therefore seem probable that some general feeling of brother-hood will grow among men, and some general recognition of God as the Source of all Life, and the Revealer of all Truth, through His Son ; and the Worker in every one through His indwelling Spirit. We shall, I believe, become through scientific methods assured that we are parts of a whole which is realising itself, in us and without us ; and this assurance is a solid basis for the reception of religious truth.

There is, lastly, a new science coming to its birth, the scientific study of the nature and the value of religious experience, of which we have received the latest instalment in Professor James's *Gifford Lectures*. What is to be the attitude of religious men towards this new

[1] *Methods of Ethics*, p. 474, ed. 1874.

science?   A saying of Agassiz is the best
indication what that attitude ought not to be.
He said that the reception of scientific dis-
coveries generally passed through three stages:
first, men said, "It is not true"; next, "It is
contrary to religion"; and then, "Everybody
knew it before."   It may be hoped that the
effect of scientific training on us all will prevent
our receiving this new science in this old
spirit.   We may be sure that so far as our
faith is in correspondence with truth and
reality it will be able to absorb all new truth
which may be laid open to us; and it cannot
be in the interest of the truth to avoid
examination; nor in the interest of light to
prefer darkness.

No scientific training and no scientific
results can ever obscure our inner conviction
of the need of righteousness, and of the
supremacy of the moral law; and if scientific
training tends to enthrone this law as supreme
in our lives, we may welcome it as a great
educator of the mind of man for the reception
of religious truth.

Printed by R. & R. CLARK, LIMITED, *Edinburgh*.

A Catalogue

of

Theological Works

published by

Macmillan & Co., Ltd.

St. Martin's Street
London, W.C.

CONTENTS

THEOLOGICAL CATALOGUE

The Bible

HISTORY OF THE BIBLE

THE BIBLE IN THE CHURCH. By Right Rev. Bishop WEST-COTT. 10th Edition. Pott 8vo. 4s. 6d.

BIBLICAL HISTORY

THE HOLY BIBLE. (Eversley Edition.) Arranged in Paragraphs, with an Introduction. By J. W. MACKAIL, M.A. 8 vols. Globe 8vo. 4s. net each.

Vol. I. Genesis—Numbers. II. Deuteronomy—2 Samuel. III. 1 Kings—Esther. IV. Job—Song of Solomon. V. Isaiah—Lamentations. VI. Ezekiel—Malachi. VII. Matthew—John. VIII. Acts—Revelation.

THE MODERN READER'S BIBLE. A Series of Books from the Sacred Scriptures presented in Modern Literary Form. The Text is that of the Revised Version. It is used by special permission of the University Presses of Oxford and Cambridge. Edited by R. G. MOULTON, M.A. Pott 8vo. 2s. 6d. each volume.

HISTORY SERIES, 6 volumes.—Genesis, The Exodus, Deuteronomy, The Judges, The Kings, The Chronicles.

POETRY SERIES, 3 volumes.—The Psalms and Lamentations, 2 vols. Biblical Idylls—Solomon's Song, Ruth, Esther, Tobit.

WISDOM SERIES, 4 volumes.—The Proverbs, Ecclesiasticus, Ecclesiastes and the Wisdom of Solomon, The Book of Job.

PROPHECY SERIES, 4 volumes.—Isaiah, Jeremiah, Ezekiel, Daniel.

NEW TESTAMENT SERIES, 4 volumes.—St. Matthew and St. Mark and the General Epistles; The Gospel, Epistles, and Revelation of St. John. St. Luke and St. Paul, 2 vols.

INTRODUCTORY SERIES, 3 volumes.—Bible Stories (Old Testament), Bible Stories (New Testament), Select Masterpieces of Biblical Literature.

ST. JAMES'S GAZETTE.—"While the sacred text has in no way been tampered with, the books are presented in modern literary form and are furnished with an introduction and notes by Professor Richard G. Moulton. The notes are scholarly, and of real help to the student."

BIBLE LESSONS. By Rev. E. A. ABBOTT, D.D. Crown 8vo. 4s. 6d.

SIDE-LIGHTS UPON BIBLE HISTORY. By Mrs. SYDNEY BUXTON. Illustrated. Crown 8vo. 5s.

STORIES FROM THE BIBLE. By Rev. A. J. CHURCH. Illustrated. Two Series. Crown 8vo. 3s. 6d. each.

BIBLE READINGS SELECTED FROM THE PENTATEUCH AND THE BOOK OF JOSHUA. By Rev. J. A. CROSS. 2nd Edition. Globe 8vo. 2s. 6d.

CHILDREN'S TREASURY OF BIBLE STORIES. By Mrs. H. GASKOIN. Pott 8vo. 1s. each. Part I. Old Testament; II. New Testament; III. Three Apostles.

THE NATIONS AROUND ISRAEL. By A. KEARY. Cr. 8vo. 3s. 6d.

Biblical History—*continued.*

VILLAGE SERMONS. By Rev. F. J. A. HORT, D.D. 8vo. 6s.

This Volume contains a Series of Sermons dealing in a popular way with the successive Books of which the Bible is made up. They form an admirable introduction to the subject.

SERMONS ON THE BOOKS OF THE BIBLE. (Selected from *Village Sermons.*) Crown 8vo. 3s. 6d.

HISTORY, PROPHECY, AND THE MONUMENTS, OR, ISRAEL AND THE NATIONS. By Prof. J. F. M'CURDY. 3 Vols. 8vo. 14s. net each. Vol. I. To the Downfall of Samaria. Vol. II. To the Fall of Nineveh. Vol. III. Completing the Work.

AMERICAN HISTORICAL REVIEW.—"His method is to interweave the histories of the connected peoples in each period, to point out the historical presuppositions and moral principles in the prophetic writings, and to treat the social constitution in separate sections. This method has obvious advantages in the hands of a competent scholar and good writer, and is employed by Mr. M'Curdy with excellent effect. His presentation of the material is admirable in arrangement; his style, though somewhat formal and Gibbonesque, is clear and picturesque."

TIMES.—"A learned treatise on the ancient history of the Semitic peoples as interpreted by the new light obtained from the modern study of their monuments."

EXPOSITORY TIMES.—"The work is very able and very welcome. . . . It will take the place of all existing histories of these nations."

A CLASS-BOOK OF OLD TESTAMENT HISTORY. By Rev. Canon MACLEAR. With Four Maps. Pott 8vo. 4s. 6d.

A CLASS-BOOK OF NEW TESTAMENT HISTORY. Including the connection of the Old and New Testament. By the same. Pott 8vo. 5s. 6d.

A SHILLING BOOK OF OLD TESTAMENT HISTORY. By the same. Pott 8vo. 1s.

A SHILLING BOOK OF NEW TESTAMENT HISTORY. By the same. Pott 8vo. 1s.

THE BIBLE FOR HOME READING. Edited, with Comments and Reflections for the use of Jewish Parents and Children, by C. G. MONTEFIORE. Part I. TO THE SECOND VISIT OF NEHEMIAH TO JERUSALEM. 2nd Edition. Extra Crown 8vo. 4s. 6d. net. Part II. Containing Selections from the Wisdom Literature, the Prophets, and the Psalter, together with extracts from the Apocrypha. Extra Crown 8vo. 5s. 6d. net.

JEWISH CHRONICLE.—"By this remarkable work Mr. Claude Montefiore has put the seal on his reputation. He has placed himself securely in the front rank of contemporary teachers of religion. He has produced at once a most original, a most instructive, and almost spiritual treatise, which will long leave its ennobling mark on Jewish religious thought in England. . . . Though the term 'epoch-making' is often misapplied, we do not hesitate to apply it on this occasion. We cannot but believe that a new era may dawn in the interest shown by Jews in the Bible."

THE OLD TESTAMENT

SCRIPTURE READINGS FOR SCHOOLS AND FAMILIES. By C. M. YONGE. Globe 8vo. 1s. 6d. each; also with comments, 3s. 6d. each.—First Series: GENESIS TO DEUTERONOMY.—Second Series: JOSHUA TO SOLOMON.—Third Series: KINGS AND THE PROPHETS.—Fourth Series: THE GOSPEL TIMES.—Fifth Series: APOSTOLIC TIMES.

The Old Testament—*continued.*

THE DIVINE LIBRARY OF THE OLD TESTAMENT. Its Origin, Preservation, Inspiration, and Permanent Value. By Rev. A. F. KIRKPATRICK, B.D. Crown 8vo. 3s. net.

TIMES.—" An eloquent and temperate plea for the critical study of the Scriptures."
MANCHESTER GUARDIAN.—" An excellent introduction to the modern view of the Old Testament. . . . The learned author is a genuine critic. . . . He expounds clearly what has been recently called the 'Analytic' treatment of the books of the Old Testament, and generally adopts its results. . . . The volume is admirably suited to fulfil its purpose of familiarising the minds of earnest Bible readers with the work which Biblical criticism is now doing."

THE DOCTRINE OF THE PROPHETS. Warburtonian Lectures 1886-1890. By Rev. A. F. KIRKPATRICK, B.D. 3rd Edition. Crown 8vo. 6s.

SCOTSMAN.—" This volume gives us the result of ripe scholarship and competent learning in a very attractive form. It is written simply, clearly, and eloquently ; and it invests the subject of which it treats with a vivid and vital interest which will commend it to the reader of general intelligence, as well as to those who are more especially occupied with such studies."
GLASGOW HERALD.—" Professor Kirkpatrick's book will be found of great value for purposes of study."
BOOKMAN.—" As a summary of the main results of recent investigation, and as a thoughtful appreciation of both the human and divine sides of the prophets' work and message, it is worth the attention of all Bible students."

THE PATRIARCHS AND LAWGIVERS OF THE OLD TESTAMENT. By FREDERICK DENISON MAURICE. New Edition. Crown 8vo. 3s. 6d.

THE PROPHETS AND KINGS OF THE OLD TESTAMENT. By the same. New Edition. Crown 8vo. 3s. 6d.

THE CANON OF THE OLD TESTAMENT. An Essay on the Growth and Formation of the Hebrew Canon of Scripture. By the Right Rev. H. E. RYLE, Bishop of Winchester. 2nd Ed. Cr. 8vo. 6s.

This edition has been carefully revised throughout, but only two substantial changes have been found necessary. An Appendix has been added to Chapter IV., dealing with the subject of the Samaritan version of the Pentateuch ; and Excursus C (dealing with the Hebrew Scriptures) has been completely re-written on the strength of valuable material kindly supplied to the author by Dr. Ginsburg.

EXPOSITOR.—" Scholars are indebted to Professor Ryle for having given them for the first time a complete and trustworthy history of the Old Testament Canon."
EXPOSITORY TIMES.—" He rightly claims that his book possesses that most English of virtues—it may be read throughout. . . . An extensive and minute research lies concealed under a most fresh and flexible English style."

THE MYTHS OF ISRAEL. THE ANCIENT BOOK OF GENESIS. WITH ANALYSIS AND EXPLANATION OF ITS COMPOSITION. By AMOS KIDDER FISKE, Author of " The Jewish Scriptures," etc. Crown 8vo. 6s.

THE EARLY NARRATIVES OF GENESIS. By the Right Rev. H. E. RYLE, Bishop of Winchester. Cr. 8vo. 3s. net.

PHILO AND HOLY SCRIPTURE, OR THE QUOTATIONS OF PHILO FROM THE BOOKS OF THE OLD TESTAMENT. With Introduction and Notes by the Right Rev. H. E. RYLE, Bishop of Winchester. Cr. 8vo. 10s. net.

In the present work the attempt has been made to collect, arrange in order, and for the first time print in full all the actual quotations from the

B

The Old Testament—*continued.*

books of the Old Testament to be found in Philo's writings, and a few of his paraphrases. For the purpose of giving general assistance to students Dr. Ryle has added footnotes, dealing principally with the text of Philo's quotations compared with that of the Septuagint; and in the introduction he has endeavoured to explain Philo's attitude towards Holy Scripture, and the character of the variations of his text from that of the Septuagint.

TIMES.—"This book will be found by students to be a very useful supplement and companion to the learned Dr. Drummond's important work, *Philo Judæus.*"

The Pentateuch—

AN HISTORICO-CRITICAL INQUIRY INTO THE ORIGIN AND COMPOSITION OF THE HEXATEUCH (PENTATEUCH AND BOOK OF JOSHUA). By Prof. A. KUENEN. Translated by PHILIP H. WICKSTEED, M.A. 8vo. 14s.

The Psalms—

THE PSALMS CHRONOLOGICALLY ARRANGED. An Amended Version, with Historical Introductions and Explanatory Notes. By Four Friends. New Edition. Crown 8vo. 5s. net.

SPECTATOR.—"One of the most instructive and valuable books that has been published for many years. It gives the Psalms a perfectly fresh setting, adds a new power of vision to the grandest poetry of nature ever produced, a new depth of lyrical pathos to the poetry of national joy, sorrow, and hope, and a new intensity of spiritual light to the divine subject of every ejaculation of praise and every invocation of want. We have given but imperfect illustrations of the new beauty and light which the translators pour upon the most perfect devotional poetry of any day or nation, and which they pour on it in almost every page, by the scholarship and perfect taste with which they have executed their work. We can only say that their version deserves to live long and to pass through many editions."

GOLDEN TREASURY PSALTER. The Student's Edition. Being an Edition with briefer Notes of "The Psalms Chronologically Arranged by Four Friends." Pott 8vo. 2s. 6d. net.

THE PSALMS. With Introductions and Critical Notes. By A. C. JENNINGS, M.A., and W. H. LOWE, M.A. In 2 vols. 2nd Edition. Crown 8vo. 10s. 6d. each.

THE BOOK OF PSALMS. Edited with Comments and Reflections for the Use of Jewish Parents and Children. By C. G. MONTE-FIORE. Crown 8vo. 1s. net.

THE PRAYER-BOOK PSALMS. Relieved of Obscurities, and made smoother for Chanting, with scarcely noticeable alteration. By the Rev. E. D. CREE, M.A. Fcap. 8vo. 2s. net.

Isaiah—

ISAIAH XL.—LXVI. With the Shorter Prophecies allied to it. By MATTHEW ARNOLD. With Notes. Crown 8vo. 5s.

A BIBLE-READING FOR SCHOOLS. The Great Prophecy of Israel's Restoration (Isaiah xl.-lxvi.) Arranged and Edited for Young Learners. By the same. 4th Edition. Pott 8vo. 1s.

Zechariah—

THE HEBREW STUDENT'S COMMENTARY ON ZECHARIAH, Hebrew and LXX. By W. H. LOWE, M.A. 8vo. 10s. 6d.

THE NEW TESTAMENT

THE AKHMIM FRAGMENT OF THE APOCRYPHAL GOSPEL OF ST. PETER. By H. B. SWETE, D.D. 8vo. 5s. net.

THE PROGRESS OF DOCTRINE IN THE NEW TESTAMENT : The Bampton Lectures, 1864. By Canon THOMAS DEHANY BERNARD, M.A. Fifth Edition. Crown 8vo. 6s.

HANDBOOK TO THE TEXTUAL CRITICISM OF NEW TESTAMENT. By F. G. KENYON, D.Litt., Assistant Keeper of Manuscripts in the British Museum. 8vo. 10s. net.

THE RISE OF THE NEW TESTAMENT. By DAVID SAVILLE MUZZEY, B.D. Fcap. 8vo. 5s.

IMMANUEL KANT.—" The Rise of the Bible as the people's book is the greatest blessing that the human race has ever experienced."

THE SOTERIOLOGY OF THE NEW TESTAMENT. By W. P. DU BOSE, M.A. Crown 8vo. 7s. 6d.

THE MESSAGES OF THE BOOKS. Being Discourses and Notes on the Books of the New Testament. By Dean FARRAR. 8vo. 14s.

ON A FRESH REVISION OF THE ENGLISH NEW TESTAMENT. With an Appendix on the last Petition of the Lord's Prayer. By Bishop LIGHTFOOT. Crown 8vo. 7s. 6d.

DISSERTATIONS ON THE APOSTOLIC AGE. By Bishop LIGHTFOOT. 8vo. 14s.

BIBLICAL ESSAYS. By Bishop LIGHTFOOT. 8vo. 12s.

THE UNITY OF THE NEW TESTAMENT. By F. D. MAURICE. 2nd Edition. 2 vols. Crown 8vo. 12s.

A GENERAL SURVEY OF THE HISTORY OF THE CANON OF THE NEW TESTAMENT DURING THE FIRST FOUR CENTURIES. By Right Rev. Bishop WESTCOTT. 7th Edition. Crown 8vo. 10s. 6d.

THE STUDENT'S LIFE OF JESUS. By G. H. GILBERT, Ph.D. Crown 8vo. 5s. net.

THE STUDENT'S LIFE OF PAUL. By G. H. GILBERT, Ph.D. Crown 8vo. 5s. net.

THE REVELATION OF JESUS : A Study of the Primary Sources of Christianity. By G. H. GILBERT, Ph.D. Crown 8vo. 5s. net.

THE FIRST INTERPRETERS OF JESUS. By G. H. GILBERT, Ph.D. Crown 8vo. 5s. net.

NEW TESTAMENT HANDBOOKS. Edited by SHAILER MATHEWS, Professor of New Test. Hist. at the University of Chicago.

A HISTORY OF NEW TESTAMENT TIMES IN PALESTINE (175 B.C.–70 A.D.). By SHAILER MATHEWS, A.M. Crown 8vo. 3s. 6d.

A HISTORY OF THE TEXTUAL CRITICISM OF THE NEW TESTAMENT. By MARVIN R. VINCENT, D.D. Crown 8vo. 3s. 6d.

THE BIBLICAL THEOLOGY OF THE NEW TESTAMENT. By EZRA P. GOULD, D.D. Crown 8vo. 3s. 6d.

A HISTORY OF THE HIGHER CRITICISM OF THE NEW TESTAMENT. By Prof. H. S. NASH. 3s. 6d.

AN INTRODUCTION TO THE NEW TESTAMENT. By B. W. BACON, D.D. Crown 8vo. 3s. 6d.

The New Testament—*continued.*

THE TEACHING OF JESUS. By G. B. Stevens, D.D. Crown
8vo. 3s. 6d.

THE NEW TESTAMENT IN THE ORIGINAL GREEK. The
Text revised by Bishop Westcott, D.D., and Prof. F. J. A.
Hort, D.D. 2 vols. Crown 8vo. 10s. 6d. each.—Vol. I.
Text; II. Introduction and Appendix.
Library Edition. 8vo. 10s. net. [*Text in Macmillan Greek Type.*
School Edition. 12mo, cloth, 4s. 6d.; roan, 5s. 6d.; morocco,
6s. 6d.; India Paper Edition, limp calf, 7s. 6d. net.

GREEK-ENGLISH LEXICON TO THE NEW TESTAMENT.
By W. J. Hickie, M.A. Pott 8vo. 3s.

ACADEMY.—"We can cordially recommend this as a very handy little volume
compiled on sound principles."

GRAMMAR OF NEW TESTAMENT GREEK. By Prof. F.
Blass, University of Halle. Auth. English Trans. 8vo. 14s. net.

TIMES.—"Will probably become the standard book of reference for those students
who enter upon minute grammatical study of the language of the New Testament."

THE GOSPELS—

PHILOLOGY OF THE GOSPELS. By Prof. F. Blass. Crown
8vo. 4s. 6d. net.

GUARDIAN.—"On the whole, Professor Blass's new book seems to us an important contribution to criticism. . . . It will stimulate inquiry, and will open up fresh
lines of thought to any serious student."

THE SYRO-LATIN TEXT OF THE GOSPELS. By the Rev.
Frederic Henry Chase, D.D. 8vo. 7s. 6d. net.

The sequel of an essay by Dr. Chase on the old Syriac element in the
text of Codex Bezae.

TIMES.—"An important and scholarly contribution to New Testament criticism."

SYNOPTICON: An Exposition of the Common Matter of the Synop-
tic Gospels. By W. G. Rushbrooke. Printed in Colours. 4to.
35s. net. Indispensable to a Theological Student.

A SYNOPSIS OF THE GOSPELS IN GREEK AFTER THE
WESTCOTT AND HORT TEXT. By Rev. Arthur Wright,
M.A. Demy 4to. 6s. net.

"Every such effort calls attention to facts which must not be overlooked, but yet to
the scholar they are but as dust in the balance when weighed against such solid con-
tributions as Rushbrooke's *Synopticon* or Wright's *Synopsis*, which provide instruments for
investigation apart from theories."—Prof. A. Robinson at Church Congress, Bradford, 1898.

THE COMPOSITION OF THE FOUR GOSPELS. By Rev.
Arthur Wright. Crown 8vo. 5s.

CAMBRIDGE REVIEW.—"The wonderful force and freshness which we find on
every page of the book. There is no sign of hastiness. All seems to be the outcome of
years of reverent thought, now brought to light in the clearest, most telling way. . . .
The book will hardly go unchallenged by the different schools of thought, but all will
agree in gratitude at least for its vigour and reality."

INTRODUCTION TO THE STUDY OF THE FOUR GOSPELS.
By Right Rev. Bishop Westcott. 8th Ed. Cr. 8vo. 10s. 6d.

FOUR LECTURES ON THE EARLY HISTORY OF THE
GOSPELS. By the Rev. J. H. Wilkinson, M.A., Rector of
Stock Gaylard, Dorset. Crown 8vo. 3s. net.

THE LEADING IDEAS OF THE GOSPELS. By W. Alex-
ander, D.D. Oxon., LL.D. Dublin, D.C.L. Oxon., Archbishop of
Armagh, and Lord Primate of All Ireland. New Edition, Revised
and Enlarged. Crown 8vo. 6s.

The Gospels—*continued.*

BRITISH WEEKLY.—"Really a new book. It sets before the reader with delicacy of thought and felicity of language the distinguishing characteristics of the several gospels. It is delightful reading. . . . Religious literature does not often furnish a book which may so confidently be recommended."

TWO LECTURES ON THE GOSPELS. By F. CRAWFORD BURKITT, M.A. Crown 8vo. 2s. 6d. net.

Gospel of St. Matthew—

THE GOSPEL ACCORDING TO ST. MATTHEW. Greek Text as Revised by Bishop WESTCOTT and Dr. HORT. With Introduction and Notes by Rev. A. SLOMAN, M.A. Fcap. 8vo. 2s. 6d.

MANCHESTER GUARDIAN.—"It is sound and helpful, and the brief introduction on Hellenistic Greek is particularly good."

Gospel of St. Mark—

THE GREEK TEXT. With Introduction, Notes, and Indices. By Rev. H. B. SWETE, D.D., Regius Professor of Divinity in the University of Cambridge. 2nd Edition. 8vo. 15s.

TIMES.—"A learned and scholarly performance, up to date with the most recent advances in New Testament criticism."

THE EARLIEST GOSPEL. A Historico-Critical Commentary on the Gospel according to St. Mark, with Text, Translation, and Introduction. By ALLAN MENZIES, Professor of Divinity and Biblical Criticism, St. Mary's College, St. Andrews. 8vo. 8s. 6d. net.

SCHOOL READINGS IN THE GREEK TESTAMENT. Being the Outlines of the Life of our Lord as given by St. Mark, with additions from the Text of the other Evangelists. Edited, with Notes and Vocabulary, by Rev. A. CALVERT, M.A. Fcap. 8vo. 2s. 6d.

Gospel of St. Luke—

THE GOSPEL ACCORDING TO ST. LUKE. The Greek Text as Revised by Bishop WESTCOTT and Dr. HORT. With Introduction and Notes by Rev. J. BOND, M.A. Fcap. 8vo. 2s. 6d.

GLASGOW HERALD.—"The notes are short and crisp—suggestive rather than exhaustive."

THE GOSPEL OF THE KINGDOM OF HEAVEN. A Course of Lectures on the Gospel of St. Luke. By F. D. MAURICE. Crown 8vo. 3s. 6d.

THE GOSPEL ACCORDING TO ST. LUKE IN GREEK, AFTER THE WESTCOTT AND HORT TEXT. Edited, with Parallels, Illustrations, Various Readings, and Notes, by the Rev. ARTHUR WRIGHT, M.A. Demy 4to. 7s. 6d. net.

ST. LUKE THE PROPHET. By EDWARD CARUS SELWYN, D.D. [Crown 8vo. 8s. 6d. net.

Gospel of St. John—

THE CENTRAL TEACHING OF CHRIST. Being a Study and Exposition of St. John, Chapters XIII. to XVII. By Rev. CANON BERNARD, M.A. Crown 8vo. 7s. 6d.

EXPOSITORY TIMES.—"Quite recently we have had an exposition by him whom many call the greatest expositor living. But Canon Bernard's work is still the work that will help the preacher most."

THE GOSPEL OF ST. JOHN. By F. D. MAURICE. Cr. 8vo. 3s. 6d.

THE ACTS OF THE APOSTLES.

ADDRESSES ON THE ACTS OF THE APOSTLES. By the late ARCHBISHOP BENSON. With an Introduction by ADELINE, DUCHESS OF BEDFORD. Super Royal 8vo. 21s. net.

THE CREDIBILITY OF THE BOOK OF THE ACTS OF THE APOSTLES. Being the Hulsean Lectures for 1900-1. By the Rev. Dr. CHASE, President of Queen's College, Cambridge. Crown 8vo. 6s.

THE OLD SYRIAC ELEMENT IN THE TEXT OF THE CODEX BEZAE. By the Rev. F. H. CHASE, D.D. 8vo. 7s. 6d. net.

THE ACTS OF THE APOSTLES IN GREEK AND ENGLISH. With Notes by Rev. F. RENDALL, M.A. Cr. 8vo. 6s.

SATURDAY REVIEW.—"Mr. Rendall has given us a very useful as well as a very scholarly book."

MANCHESTER GUARDIAN.—"Mr. Rendall is a careful scholar and a thoughtful writer, and the student may learn a good deal from his commentary."

THE ACTS OF THE APOSTLES. By F. D. MAURICE. Cr. 8vo. 3s. 6d.

THE ACTS OF THE APOSTLES. Being the Greek Text as Revised by Bishop WESTCOTT and Dr. HORT. With Explanatory Notes by T. E. PAGE, M.A. Fcap. 8vo. 3s. 6d.

ACTS OF THE APOSTLES. The Authorised Version, with Introduction and Notes, by T. E. PAGE, M.A., and Rev. A. S. WALPOLE, M.A. Fcap. 8vo. 2s. 6d.

BRITISH WEEKLY.—"Mr. Page's Notes on the Greek Text of the Acts are very well known, and are decidedly scholarly and individual. . . . Mr. Page has written an introduction which is brief, scholarly, and suggestive."

THE CHURCH OF THE FIRST DAYS. THE CHURCH OF JERUSALEM. THE CHURCH OF THE GENTILES. THE CHURCH OF THE WORLD. Lectures on the Acts of the Apostles. By Very Rev. C. J. VAUGHAN. Crown 8vo. 10s. 6d.

THE EPISTLES—The Epistles of St. Paul—

ST. PAUL'S EPISTLE TO THE ROMANS. The Greek Text, with English Notes. By Very Rev. C. J. VAUGHAN. 7th Edition. Crown 8vo. 7s. 6d.

ST. PAUL'S EPISTLE TO THE ROMANS. A New Translation by Rev. W. G. RUTHERFORD. 8vo. 3s. 6d. net.

PILOT.—"Small as the volume is, it has very much to say, not only to professed students of the New Testament, but also to the ordinary reader of the Bible. . . . The layman who buys the book will be grateful to one who helps him to realise that this perplexing Epistle 'was once a plain letter concerned with a theme which plain men might understand.'"

PROLEGOMENA TO ST. PAUL'S EPISTLES TO THE ROMANS AND THE EPHESIANS. By Rev. F. J. A. HORT. Crown 8vo. 6s.

Dr. MARCUS DODS in the *Bookman.*—"Anything from the pen of Dr. Hort is sure to be informative and suggestive, and the present publication bears his mark. . . . There is an air of originality about the whole discussion; the difficulties are candidly faced, and the explanations offered appeal to our sense of what is reasonable."

TIMES.—"Will be welcomed by all theologians as 'an invaluable contribution to the study of those Epistles' as the editor of the volume justly calls it."

DAILY CHRONICLE.—"The lectures are an important contribution to the study of the famous Epistles of which they treat."

The Epistles of St. Paul—*continued.*

THE EPISTLE TO THE GALATIANS. An Essay on its Destination and Date. By E. H. ASKWITH, D.D. Crown 8vo. 3s. 6d. net.

ST. PAUL'S EPISTLE TO THE GALATIANS. A Revised Text, with Introduction, Notes, and Dissertations. By Bishop LIGHTFOOT. 10th Edition. 8vo. 12s.

ST. PAUL'S EPISTLE TO THE EPHESIANS. The Greek Text with Notes. By the late Bishop WESTCOTT. [*In the Press.*

ST. PAUL'S EPISTLE TO THE EPHESIANS. Greek Text, with Introduction and Notes. By Dean ROBINSON. 8vo. [*In the Press.*

ST. PAUL'S EPISTLE TO THE PHILIPPIANS. A Revised Text, with Introduction, Notes, and Dissertations. By Bishop LIGHTFOOT. 9th Edition. 8vo. 12s.

ST. PAUL'S EPISTLE TO THE PHILIPPIANS. With translation, Paraphrase, and Notes for English Readers. By Very Rev. C. J. VAUGHAN. Crown 8vo. 5s.

ST. PAUL'S EPISTLES TO THE COLOSSIANS AND TO PHILEMON. A Revised Text, with Introductions, etc. By Bishop LIGHTFOOT. 9th Edition. 8vo. 12s.

THE EPISTLE TO THE COLOSSIANS. Analysis and Examination Notes. By Rev. G. W. GARROD. Crown 8vo. 3s. net.

AN INTRODUCTION TO THE THESSALONIAN EPISTLES. By E. H. ASKWITH, D.D., Chaplain of Trinity College, Cambridge. Crown 8vo. 4s. net.

THE FIRST EPISTLE TO THE THESSALONIANS. With Analysis and Notes by the Rev. G. W. GARROD, B.A. Crown 8vo. 2s. 6d. net.

THE SECOND EPISTLE TO THE THESSALONIANS. With Analysis and Notes by Rev. G. W. GARROD. Cr. 8vo. 2s. 6d. net.

THE EPISTLES OF ST. PAUL TO THE EPHESIANS, THE COLOSSIANS, AND PHILEMON. With Introductions and Notes. By Rev. J. LL. DAVIES. 2nd Edition. 8vo. 7s. 6d.

THE EPISTLES OF ST. PAUL. For English Readers. Part I. containing the First Epistle to the Thessalonians. By Very Rev. C. J. VAUGHAN. 2nd Edition. 8vo. Sewed. 1s. 6d.

NOTES ON EPISTLES OF ST. PAUL FROM UNPUBLISHED COMMENTARIES. By Bishop LIGHTFOOT, D.D. 8vo. 12s.

THE LETTERS OF ST. PAUL TO SEVEN CHURCHES AND THREE FRIENDS. Translated by ARTHUR S. WAY, M.A. Crown 8vo. 5s. net.

The Epistles of St. Peter—

THE FIRST EPISTLE OF ST. PETER, I. 1 to II. 17. The Greek Text, with Introductory Lecture, Commentary, and additional Notes. By the late F. J. A. HORT, D.D., D.C.L., LL.D. 8vo. 6s.

The Epistles of St. Peter—*continued*.

THE FIRST EPISTLE OF ST. PETER (Greek Text). By J. Howard B. Masterman, Principal of the Midland Clergy College, Edgbaston, Birmingham. Crown 8vo. 3s. 6d. net.

The Epistle of St. James—

THE EPISTLE OF ST. JAMES. The Greek Text, with Introduction and Notes. By Rev. Joseph B. Mayor, M.A. 2nd Edition. 8vo. 14s. net.

EXPOSITORY TIMES.—"The most complete edition of St. James in the English language, and the most serviceable for the student of Greek."

BOOKMAN.—"Professor Mayor's volume in every part of it gives proof that no time or labour has been grudged in mastering this mass of literature, and that in appraising it he has exercised the sound judgment of a thoroughly trained scholar and critic. . . . The notes are uniformly characterised by thorough scholarship and unfailing sense. The notes resemble rather those of Lightfoot than those of Ellicott. . . . It is a pleasure to welcome a book which does credit to English learning, and which will take, and keep, a foremost place in Biblical literature."

SCOTSMAN.—"It is a work which sums up many others, and to any one who wishes to make a thorough study of the Epistle of St. James, it will prove indispensable."

EXPOSITOR (Dr. Marcus Dods).—"Will long remain the commentary on St. James, a storehouse to which all subsequent students of the epistle must be indebted."

The Epistles of St. John—

THE EPISTLES OF ST. JOHN. By F. D. Maurice. Crown 8vo. 3s. 6d.

THE EPISTLES OF ST. JOHN. The Greek Text, with Notes. By Right Rev. Bishop Westcott. 4th Edition. 8vo. 12s. 6d.

GUARDIAN.—"It contains a new or rather revised text, with careful critical remarks and helps; very copious footnotes on the text; and after each of the chapters, longer and more elaborate notes in treatment of leading or difficult questions, whether in respect of reading or theology. . . . Dr. Westcott has accumulated round them so much matter that, if not new, was forgotten, or generally unobserved, and has thrown so much light upon their language, theology, and characteristics. . . . The notes, critical, illustrative, and exegetical, which are given beneath the text, are extraordinarily full and careful. . . . They exhibit the same minute analysis of every phrase and word, the same scrupulous weighing of every inflection and variation that characterised Dr. Westcott's commentary on the Gospel. . . . There is scarcely a syllable throughout the Epistles which is dismissed without having undergone the most anxious interrogation."

SATURDAY REVIEW.—"The more we examine this precious volume the more its exceeding richness in spiritual as well as in literary material grows upon the mind."

The Epistle to the Hebrews—

THE EPISTLE TO THE HEBREWS IN GREEK AND ENGLISH. With Notes. By Rev. F. Rendall. Cr. 8vo. 6s.

THE EPISTLE TO THE HEBREWS. English Text, with Commentary. By the same. Crown 8vo. 7s. 6d.

THE EPISTLE TO THE HEBREWS. With Notes. By Very Rev. C. J. Vaughan. Crown 8vo. 7s. 6d.

TIMES.—"The name and reputation of the Dean of Llandaff are a better recommendation than we can give of the *Epistle to the Hebrews*, the Greek text, with notes; an edition which represents the results of more than thirty years' experience in the training of students for ordination."

THE EPISTLE TO THE HEBREWS. The Greek Text, with Notes and Essays. By Right Rev. Bishop Westcott. 8vo. 14s.

GUARDIAN.—"In form this is a companion volume to that upon the Epistles of St. John. The type is excellent, the printing careful, the index thorough; and the volume contains a full introduction, followed by the Greek text, with a running commentary, and a number of additional notes on verbal and doctrinal points which needed fuller discussion. . . . His conception of inspiration is further illustrated by the treatment of the Old Testament in the Epistle, and the additional notes that bear on this point deserve very careful study. The spirit in which the student should approach the perplexing questions of Old Testament criticism could not be better described than it is in the last essay."

The Book of Revelations—

THE APOCALYPSE. A Study. By ARCHBISHOP BENSON. 8vo. 8s. 6d. net.

LECTURES ON THE APOCALYPSE. By Rev. Prof. W. MILLIGAN. Crown 8vo. 5s.

DISCUSSIONS ON THE APOCALYPSE. By the same. Cr. 8vo. 5s.

SCOTSMAN.—" These discussions give an interesting and valuable account and criticism of the present state of theological opinion and research in connection with their subject."

SCOTTISH GUARDIAN.—" The great merit of the book is the patient and skilful way in which it has brought the whole discussion down to the present day. . . . The result is a volume which many will value highly, and which will not, we think, soon be superseded."

LECTURES ON THE REVELATION OF ST. JOHN. By Very Rev. C. J. VAUGHAN. 5th Edition. Crown 8vo. 10s. 6d.

THE CHRISTIAN PROPHETS AND THE PROPHETIC APOCALYPSE. By EDWARD CARUS SELWYN, D.D. Crown 8vo. 6s. net.

THE BIBLE WORD-BOOK. By W. ALDIS WRIGHT, Litt.D., LL.D. 2nd Edition. Crown 8vo. 7s. 6d.

Christian Church, History of the

Cheetham (Archdeacon).—A HISTORY OF THE CHRISTIAN CHURCH DURING THE FIRST SIX CENTURIES. Cr. 8vo. 10s. 6d.

TIMES.—" A brief but authoritative summary of early ecclesiastical history."

GLASGOW HERALD.—" Particularly clear in its exposition, systematic in its disposition and development, and as light and attractive in style as could reasonably be expected from the nature of the subject."

Gwatkin (H. M.)—SELECTIONS FROM EARLY WRITERS Illustrative of Church History to the Time of Constantine. 2nd Edition. Revised and Enlarged. Cr. 8vo. 4s. 6d. net.

To this edition have been prefixed short accounts of the writers from whom the passages are selected.

Hardwick (Archdeacon).—A HISTORY OF THE CHRISTIAN CHURCH. Middle Age. Ed. by Bishop STUBBS. Cr. 8vo. 10s. 6d.

A HISTORY OF THE CHRISTIAN CHURCH DURING THE REFORMATION. Revised by Bishop STUBBS. Cr. 8vo. 10s. 6d.

Hort (Dr. F. J. A.)—TWO DISSERTATIONS. I. On ΜΟΝΟΓΕΝΗΣ ΘΕΟΣ in Scripture and Tradition. II. On the "Constantinopolitan" Creed and other Eastern Creeds of the Fourth Century. 8vo. 7s. 6d.

JUDAISTIC CHRISTIANITY. Crown 8vo. 6s.

THE CHRISTIAN ECCLESIA. A Course of Lectures on the Early History and Early Conceptions of the Ecclesia, and Four Sermons. Crown 8vo. 6s.

Krüger (Dr. G.)—HISTORY OF EARLY CHRISTIAN LITERATURE IN THE FIRST THREE CENTURIES. Cr. 8vo. 8s. 6d. net.

Lowrie (W.)—CHRISTIAN ART AND ARCHÆOLOGY: A HANDBOOK TO THE MONUMENTS OF THE EARLY CHURCH. Crown 8vo. 10s. 6d.

Oliphant (T. L. Kington)—ROME AND REFORM. 2 vols. 8vo. 21s. net.

Simpson (W.)—AN EPITOME OF THE HISTORY OF THE CHRISTIAN CHURCH. Fcap. 8vo. 3s. 6d.

Sohm (Prof.) — OUTLINES OF CHURCH HISTORY. Translated by Miss MAY SINCLAIR. With a Preface by Prof. H. M. GWATKIN, M.A. Crown 8vo. 3s. 6d.

MANCHESTER GUARDIAN.—"It fully deserves the praise given to it by Professor Gwatkin (who contributes a preface to this translation) of being 'neither a meagre sketch nor a confused mass of facts, but a masterly outline,' and it really 'supplies a want,' as affording to the intelligent reader who has no time or interest in details, a connected general view of the whole vast field of ecclesiastical history."

Vaughan (Very Rev. C. J., Dean of Llandaff).—THE CHURCH OF THE FIRST DAYS. THE CHURCH OF JERUSALEM. THE CHURCH OF THE GENTILES. THE CHURCH OF THE WORLD. Crown 8vo. 10s. 6d.

The Church of England

Catechism of—

CATECHISM AND CONFIRMATION. By Rev. J. C. P. ALDOUS. Pott 8vo. 1s. net.

THOSE HOLY MYSTERIES. By Rev. J. C. P. ALDOUS. Pott 8vo. 1s. net.

A CLASS-BOOK OF THE CATECHISM OF THE CHURCH OF ENGLAND. By Rev. Canon MACLEAR. Pott 8vo. 1s. 6d.

A FIRST CLASS-BOOK OF THE CATECHISM OF THE CHURCH OF ENGLAND, with Scripture Proofs for Junior Classes and Schools. By the same. Pott 8vo. 6d.

THE ORDER OF CONFIRMATION, with Prayers and Devotions. By the Rev. Canon MACLEAR. 32mo. 6d.

NOTES FOR LECTURES ON CONFIRMATION. By the Rev. C. J. VAUGHAN, D.D. Pott 8vo. 1s. 6d.

THE BAPTISMAL OFFICE AND THE ORDER OF CONFIRMATION. By the Rev. F. PROCTER and the Rev. CANON MACLEAR. Pott 8vo. 6d.

Disestablishment—

DISESTABLISHMENT AND DISENDOWMENT. What are they? By Prof. E. A. FREEMAN. 4th Edition. Crown 8vo. 1s.

A DEFENCE OF THE CHURCH OF ENGLAND AGAINST DISESTABLISHMENT. By ROUNDELL, EARL OF SELBORNE. Crown 8vo. 2s. 6d.

ANCIENT FACTS & FICTIONS CONCERNING CHURCHES AND TITHES. By the same. 2nd Edition. Crown 8vo. 7s. 6d.

Disestablishment—*continued.*

A HANDBOOK ON WELSH CHURCH DEFENCE. By the Bishop of St. Asaph. 3rd Edition. Fcap. 8vo. Sewed, 6d.

Dissent in its Relation to—

DISSENT IN ITS RELATION TO THE CHURCH OF ENGLAND. By Rev. G. H. Curteis. Bampton Lectures for 1871. Crown 8vo. 7s. 6d.

History of—

HISTORY OF THE CHURCH OF ENGLAND. Edited by Dean Stephens and the Rev. W. Hunt. In Eight Volumes. Crown 8vo.

> Vol. I. HISTORY OF THE CHURCH OF ENGLAND PRIOR TO THE NORMAN CONQUEST. By the Rev. W. Hunt, M.A. Cr. 8vo. 7s. 6d. [*Ready.*
>
> Vol. II. THE ENGLISH CHURCH FROM THE NORMAN CONQUEST TO THE CLOSE OF THE THIRTEENTH CENTURY. By Dean Stephens. Cr. 8vo. 7s. 6d. [*Ready.*
>
> Vol. III. THE ENGLISH CHURCH IN THE FOURTEENTH AND FIFTEENTH CENTURIES (1372-1486). By the Rev. Canon Capes, sometime Reader of Ancient History in the University of Oxford. 7s. 6d. [*Ready.*
>
> Vol. IV. THE ENGLISH CHURCH IN THE SIXTEENTH CENTURY, FROM THE ACCESSION OF HENRY VIII. TO THE DEATH OF MARY. By James Gairdner, C.B., LL.D. 7s. 6d. [*Ready.*
>
> *In Preparation.*
>
> Vol. V. THE ENGLISH CHURCH IN THE REIGNS OF ELIZABETH AND JAMES I. By the Rev. W. H. Frere.
>
> Vol. VI. THE ENGLISH CHURCH FROM THE ACCESSION OF CHARLES I. TO THE DEATH OF ANNE. By the Rev. W. H. Hutton, B.D., Fellow of St. John's College, Oxford.
>
> Vol. VII. THE ENGLISH CHURCH IN THE EIGHTEENTH CENTURY. By the Rev. Canon Overton, D.D.
>
> Vol. VIII. THE ENGLISH CHURCH IN THE NINETEENTH CENTURY. By F. W. Cornish, M.A., Vice-Provost of Eton College.

THE STATE AND THE CHURCH. By the Hon. Arthur Elliot. New Edition. Crown 8vo. 2s. 6d.

DOCUMENTS ILLUSTRATIVE OF ENGLISH CHURCH HISTORY. Compiled from Original Sources by Henry Gee, B.D., F.S.A., and W. J. Hardy, F.S.A. Cr. 8vo. 10s. 6d.

ENGLISH HISTORICAL REVIEW.—"Will be welcomed alike by students and by a much wider circle of readers interested in the history of the Church of England. For the benefit of the latter all the Latin pieces have been translated into English. . . . It fully deserves the hearty imprimatur of the Bishop of Oxford prefixed to it."

DAILY CHRONICLE.—"Students of the English Constitution as well as students of Church History will find this volume a valuable aid to their researches."

SCOTTISH GUARDIAN.—"There is no book in existence that contains so much original material likely to prove valuable to those who wish to investigate ritual or historical questions affecting the English Church."

Holy Communion—

THE COMMUNION SERVICE FROM THE BOOK OF COMMON PRAYER, with Select Readings from the Writings of the Rev. F. D. MAURICE. Edited by Bishop COLENSO. 6th Edition. 16mo. 2s. 6d.

FIRST COMMUNION, with Prayers and Devotions for the newly Confirmed. By Rev. Canon MACLEAR. 32mo. 6d.

A MANUAL OF INSTRUCTION FOR CONFIRMATION AND FIRST COMMUNION, with Prayers and Devotions. By the same. 32mo. 2s.

Liturgy—

A COMPANION TO THE LECTIONARY. By Rev. W. BENHAM, B.D. Crown 8vo. 4s. 6d.

AN INTRODUCTION TO THE CREEDS. By Rev. Canon MACLEAR. Pott 8vo. 3s. 6d.

CHURCH QUARTERLY REVIEW.—"Mr. Maclear's text-books of Bible history are so well known that to praise them is unnecessary. He has now added to them *An Introduction to the Creeds*, which we do not hesitate to call admirable. The book consists, first, of an historical introduction, occupying 53 pages, then an exposition of the twelve articles of the Creed extending to page 299, an appendix containing the texts of a considerable number of Creeds, and lastly, three indices which, as far as we have tested them, we must pronounce very good. . . . We may add that we know already that the book has been used with great advantage in ordinary parochial work."

AN INTRODUCTION TO THE ARTICLES OF THE CHURCH OF ENGLAND. By Rev. G. F. MACLEAR, D.D., and Rev. W. W. WILLIAMS. Crown 8vo. 10s. 6d.

The BISHOP OF SALISBURY at the Church Congress spoke of this as "a book which will doubtless have, as it deserves, large circulation."
ST. JAMES'S GAZETTE.—"Theological students and others will find this comprehensive yet concise volume most valuable."
GLASGOW HERALD.—"A valuable addition to the well-known series of Theological Manuals published by Messrs. Macmillan."
CHURCH TIMES.—"Those who are in any way responsible for the training of candidates for Holy Orders must often have felt the want of such a book as Dr. Maclear, with the assistance of his colleague, Mr. Williams, has just published."

NEW HISTORY OF THE BOOK OF COMMON PRAYER. With a rationale of its Offices on the basis of the former Work by FRANCIS PROCTER, M.A. Revised and re-written by WALTER HOWARD FRERE, M.A., Priest of the Community of the Resurrection. Second Impression. Crown 8vo. 12s. 6d.

AN ELEMENTARY INTRODUCTION TO THE BOOK OF COMMON PRAYER. By Rev. F. PROCTER and Rev. Canon MACLEAR. Pott 8vo. 2s. 6d.

THE ELIZALETHAN PRAYER-BOOK AND ORNAMENTS. With an Appendix of Documents. By HENRY GEE, D.D. Crown 8vo. 5s.

TWELVE DISCOURSES ON SUBJECTS CONNECTED WITH THE LITURGY AND WORSHIP OF THE CHURCH OF ENGLAND. By Very Rev. C. J. VAUGHAN. 4th Edition. Fcap. 8vo. 6s.

Historical and Biographical—

THE ECCLESIASTICAL EXPANSION OF ENGLAND IN THE GROWTH OF THE ANGLICAN COMMUNION. Hulsean Lectures, 1894-95. By ALFRED BARRY, D.D., D.C.L., formerly Bishop of Sydney and Primate of Australia and Tasmania. Crown 8vo. 6s.

The author's preface says : "The one object of these lectures—delivered on the Hulsean Foundation in 1894-95—is to make some slight contribution to that awakening of interest in the extraordinary religious mission of England which seems happily characteristic of the present time."

DAILY NEWS.—"These lectures are particularly interesting as containing the case for the Christian missions at a time when there is a disposition to attack them in some quarters."

LIVES OF THE ARCHBISHOPS OF CANTERBURY. From St. Augustine to Juxon. By the Very Rev. WALTER FARQUHAR HOOK, D.D., Dean of Chichester. Demy 8vo. The volumes sold separately as follows :—Vol. I., 15s. ; Vol. II., 15s. ; Vol. V., 15s. ; Vols. VI. and VII., 30s. ; Vol. VIII., 15s. ; Vol. X., 15s. ; Vol. XI., 15s. ; Vol. XII., 15s.

ATHENÆUM.—"The most impartial, the most instructive, and the most interesting of histories."

THE LIFE OF THE RIGHT REVEREND BROOKE FOSS WESTCOTT, D.D., Late Lord Bishop of Durham. By his Son, the Rev. ARTHUR WESTCOTT. With Photogravure Portraits. 2 vols. Extra Crown 8vo. 17s. net.

LIFE AND LETTERS OF ARCHBISHOP BENSON. By his SON. Two Vols. 8vo. 36s. net.

Abridged Edition. In one Vol. 8s. 6d. net.

CHARLOTTE MARY YONGE: HER LIFE AND LETTERS. By CHRISTABEL COLERIDGE. With Portraits. 8vo. 12s. 6d. net.

LIFE AND LETTERS OF AMBROSE PHILLIPPS DE LISLE. By E. S. PURCELL. Two Vols. 8vo. 25s. net.

THE OXFORD MOVEMENT. Twelve Years, 1833-45. By DEAN CHURCH. Globe 8vo. 4s. net.

THE LIFE AND LETTERS OF R. W. CHURCH, late Dean of St. Paul's. Globe 8vo. 4s. net.

JAMES FRASER, SECOND BISHOP OF MANCHESTER. A Memoir. 1818-1885. By THOMAS HUGHES. 2nd Ed. Crown 8vo. 6s.

LIFE AND LETTERS OF FENTON JOHN ANTHONY HORT, D.D., D.C.L., LL.D., sometime Hulsean Professor and Lady Margaret's Reader in Divinity in the University of Cambridge. By his Son, ARTHUR FENTON HORT, late Fellow of Trinity College, Cambridge. In two Vols. With Portrait. Ex. Cr. 8vo. 17s. net.

EXPOSITOR.—"It is only just to publish the life of a scholar at once so well known and so little known as Dr. Hort. . . . But all who appreciate his work wish to know more, and the two fascinating volumes edited by his son give us the information we seek. They reveal to us a man the very antipodes of a dry-as-dust pedant, a man with many interests and enthusiasms, a lover of the arts and of nature, an athlete and one of the founders of the Alpine Club, a man of restless mind but always at leisure for the demands of friendship, and finding his truest joy in his own home and family."

Historical and Biographical—*continued.*

THE LIFE OF FREDERICK DENISON MAURICE. Chiefly told in his own letters. Edited by his Son, FREDERICK MAURICE. With Portraits. Two Vols. Crown 8vo. 16s.

MEMORIALS. (PART I.) FAMILY AND PERSONAL, 1766-1865. By ROUNDELL, EARL OF SELBORNE. With Portraits and Illustrations. Two Vols. 8vo. 25s. net. (PART II.) PERSONAL AND POLITICAL, 1865-1895. Two Vols. 25s. net.

LIFE OF ARCHIBALD CAMPBELL TAIT, ARCHBISHOP OF CANTERBURY. By ARCHBISHOP DAVIDSON and WILLIAM BENHAM, B.D., Hon. Canon of Canterbury. With Portraits. 3rd Edition. Two Vols. Crown 8vo. 10s.

LIFE AND LETTERS OF WILLIAM JOHN BUTLER, late Dean of Lincoln, sometime Vicar of Wantage. 8vo. 12s. 6d. net.

TIMES.—"We have a graphic picture of a strong personality, and the example of a useful and laborious life. . . . Well put together and exceedingly interesting to Churchmen."

IN THE COURT OF THE ARCHBISHOP OF CANTER-BURY. Read and others *v.* The Lord Bishop of Lincoln. Judgment, Nov. 21, 1890. 2nd Edition. 8vo. 2s. net.

THE ARCHBISHOP OF CANTERBURY ON RESERVATION OF THE SACRAMENT. Lambeth Palace, May 1, 1900. 8vo. Sewed. 1s. net.

THE ARCHBISHOP OF YORK ON RESERVATION OF SACRAMENT. Lambeth Palace, May 1, 1900. 8vo. Sewed. 1s. net.

JOURNAL OF THEOLOGICAL STUDIES. Quarterly. 3s. 6d. net. (No. 1, October 1899.)

CANTERBURY DIOCESAN GAZETTE. Monthly. 8vo. 2d.

JEWISH QUARTERLY REVIEW. Edited by I. ABRAHAMS and C. G. MONTEFIORE. Demy 8vo. 3s. 6d. Vols. 1-7, 12s. 6d. each. Vol. 8 onwards, 15s. each. (Annual Subscription, 11s.)

Devotional Books

Cornish (J. F.)—WEEK BY WEEK. Fcap. 8vo. 3s. 6d.

SPECTATOR.—"They are very terse and excellent verses, generally on the subject of either the Epistle or Gospel for the day, and are put with the kind of practical vigour which arrests attention and compels the conscience to face boldly some leading thought in the passage selected."

SATURDAY REVIEW.—"The studied simplicity of Mr. Cornish's verse is altogether opposed to what most hymn-writers consider to be poetry. Nor is this the only merit of his unpretentious volume. There is a tonic character in the exhortation and admonition that characterise the hymns, and the prevailing sentiment is thoroughly manly and rousing."

Eastlake (Lady).—FELLOWSHIP: LETTERS ADDRESSED TO MY SISTER-MOURNERS. Crown 8vo. 2s. 6d.

ATHENÆUM.—"Tender and unobtrusive, and the author thoroughly realises the sorrow of those she addresses; it may soothe mourning readers, and can by no means aggravate or jar upon their feelings."

Eastlake (Lady)—*continued.*

CONTEMPORARY REVIEW.—"A very touching and at the same time a very sensible book. It breathes throughout the truest Christian spirit."

NONCONFORMIST.—"A beautiful little volume, written with genuine feeling, good taste, and a right appreciation of the teaching of Scripture relative to sorrow and suffering."

IMITATIO CHRISTI, LIBRI IV. Printed in Borders after Holbein, Dürer, and other old Masters, containing Dances of Death, Acts of Mercy, Emblems, etc. Crown 8vo. 7s. 6d.

Keble (J.)—THE CHRISTIAN YEAR. Edited by C. M. YONGE. Pott 8vo. 2s. 6d. net.

Kingsley (Charles). — OUT OF THE DEEP : WORDS FOR THE SORROWFUL. From the writings of CHARLES KINGSLEY. Extra fcap. 8vo. 3s. 6d.

DAILY THOUGHTS. Selected from the Writings of CHARLES KINGSLEY. By his Wife. Crown 8vo. 6s.

FROM DEATH TO LIFE. Fragments of Teaching to a Village Congregation. With Letters on the "Life after Death." Edited by his Wife. Fcap. 8vo. 2s. 6d.

Maclear (Rev. Canon).—A MANUAL OF INSTRUCTION FOR CONFIRMATION AND FIRST COMMUNION, WITH PRAYERS AND DEVOTIONS. 32mo. 2s.

THE HOUR OF SORROW ; OR, THE OFFICE FOR THE BURIAL OF THE DEAD. 32mo. 2s.

Maurice (Frederick Denison).—LESSONS OF HOPE. Readings from the Works of F. D. MAURICE. Selected by Rev. J. LL. DAVIES, M.A. Crown 8vo. 5s.

THE COMMUNION SERVICE. From the Book of Common Prayer, with select readings from the writings of the Rev. F. D. MAURICE, M.A. Edited by the Rev. JOHN WILLIAM COLENSO, D.D., Lord Bishop of Natal. 16mo. 2s. 6d.

THE WORSHIP OF GOD, AND FELLOWSHIP AMONG MEN. By FREDERICK DENISON MAURICE and others. Fcap. 8vo. 3s. 6d.

RAYS OF SUNLIGHT FOR DARK DAYS. With a Preface by Very Rev. C. J. VAUGHAN, D.D. New Edition. Pott 8vo. 3s. 6d.

Welby-Gregory (The Hon. Lady).—LINKS AND CLUES. 2nd Edition. Crown 8vo. 6s.

Westcott (Bishop).—THOUGHTS ON REVELATION AND LIFE. Selections from the Writings of Bishop WESTCOTT. Edited by Rev. S. PHILLIPS. Crown 8vo. 6s.

The Fathers

INDEX OF NOTEWORTHY WORDS AND PHRASES FOUND IN THE CLEMENTINE WRITINGS, COMMONLY CALLED THE HOMILIES OF CLEMENT. 8vo. 5s.

Benson (Archbishop).—CYPRIAN : HIS LIFE, HIS TIMES, HIS WORK. By the late EDWARD WHITE BENSON, Archbishop of Canterbury. 8vo. 21s. net.

Benson (Archbishop)—*continued*.

TIMES.—"In all essential respects, in sobriety of judgment and temper, in sympathetic insight into character, in firm grasp of historical and ecclesiastical issues, in scholarship and erudition, the finished work is worthy of its subject and worthy of its author. . . . In its main outlines full of dramatic insight and force, and in its details full of the fruits of ripe learning, sound judgment, a lofty Christian temper, and a mature ecclesiastical wisdom."

SATURDAY REVIEW.—"On the whole, and with all reservations which can possibly be made, this weighty volume is a contribution to criticism and learning on which we can but congratulate the Anglican Church. We wish more of her bishops were capable or desirous of descending into that arena of pure intellect from which Dr. Benson returns with these posthumous laurels."

Gwatkin (H. M.)—SELECTIONS FROM EARLY WRITERS ILLUSTRATIVE OF CHURCH HISTORY TO THE TIME OF CONSTANTINE. 2nd Edition. Crown 8vo. 4s. 6d. net.

Hort (Dr. F. J. A.)—SIX LECTURES ON THE ANTE-NICENE FATHERS. Crown 8vo. 3s. 6d.

TIMES.—"Though certainly popular in form and treatment they are so in the best sense of the words, and they bear throughout the impress of the ripe scholarship, the rare critical acumen, and the lofty ethical temper which marked all Dr. Hort's work."

NOTES ON CLEMENTINE RECOGNITIONS. Crown 8vo. 4s. 6d.

Hort (Dr. F. J. A.) and **Mayor** (J. B.)—CLEMENT OF ALEXANDRIA: MISCELLANIES (STROMATEIS). Book VII. The Greek Text, with Introduction, Translation, Notes, Dissertations, and Indices. 8vo. 15s. net.

Krüger (G.)—HISTORY OF EARLY CHRISTIAN LITERATURE IN THE FIRST THREE CENTURIES. Crown 8vo. 8s. 6d. net.

Lightfoot (Bishop).—THE APOSTOLIC FATHERS. Part I. ST. CLEMENT OF ROME. Revised Texts, with Introductions, Notes, Dissertations, and Translations. 2 vols. 8vo. 32s.

THE APOSTOLIC FATHERS. Part II. ST. IGNATIUS to ST. POLYCARP. Revised Texts, with Introductions, Notes, Dissertations, and Translations. 3 vols. 2nd Edition. Demy 8vo. 48s.

THE APOSTOLIC FATHERS. Abridged Edition. With Short Introductions, Greek Text, and English Translation. 8vo. 16s.

MANCHESTER GUARDIAN.—"A conspectus of these early and intensely interesting Christian 'Documents' such as had not hitherto been attainable, and thereby renders a priceless service to all serious students of Christian theology, and even of Roman history."

NATIONAL OBSERVER.—"From the account of its contents, the student may appreciate the value of this last work of a great scholar, and its helpfulness as an aid to an intelligent examination of the earliest post-Apostolic writers. The texts are constructed on the most careful collation of all the existing sources. The introductions are brief, lucid, and thoroughly explanatory of the historical and critical questions related to the texts. The introduction to the *Didache*, and the translation of the 'Church Manual of Early Christianity,' are peculiarly interesting, as giving at once an admirable version of it, and the opinion of the first of English biblical critics on the latest discovery in patristic literature."

Hymnology

Bernard (Canon T. D.)—THE SONGS OF THE HOLY NATIVITY. Being Studies of the Benedictus, Magnificat, Gloria in Excelsis, and Nunc Dimittis. Crown 8vo. 5s.

Brooke (Stopford A.)—CHRISTIAN HYMNS.   Edited and arranged.   Fcap. 8vo.   2s. 6d. net.

Selborne (Roundell, Earl of)—

THE BOOK OF PRAISE.   From the best English Hymn Writers. Pott 8vo.   2s. 6d. net.

A HYMNAL.   Chiefly from *The Book of Praise.*   In various sizes. B. Pott 8vo, larger type.   1s.—C. Same Edition, fine paper.   1s. 6d.— An Edition with Music, Selected, Harmonised, and Composed by JOHN HULLAH.   Pott 8vo.   3s. 6d.

Smith (Horace).—HYMNS AND PSALMS.   Ex. Crown 8vo. 2s. 6d.

Woods (M. A.) — HYMNS FOR SCHOOL WORSHIP. Compiled by M. A. WOODS.   Pott 8vo.   1s. 6d.

Religious Teaching

Bell (Rev. G. C.)—RELIGIOUS TEACHING IN SECOND-ARY SCHOOLS.   For Teachers and Parents.   Suggestions as to Lessons on the Bible, Early Church History, Christian Evidences, etc.   By the Rev. G. C. BELL, M.A., Master of Marlborough College.   2nd Edition.   With new chapter on Christian Ethic. Crown 8vo.   3s. 6d.

GUARDIAN.—"The hints and suggestions given are admirable, and, as far as Bible teaching or instruction in 'Christian Evidences' is concerned, leave nothing to be desired. Much time and thought has evidently been devoted by the writer to the difficulties which confront the teacher of the Old Testament, and a large portion of the volume is taken up with the consideration of this branch of his subject."

EDUCATIONAL REVIEW.—"For those teachers who are dissatisfied with the existing state of things, and who are striving after something better, this little handbook is invaluable.   Its aim is 'to map out a course of instruction on practical lines, and to suggest methods and books which may point the way to a higher standpoint and a wider horizon.'   For the carrying out of this, and also for his criticism of prevailing methods, all teachers owe Mr. Bell a debt of gratitude; and if any are roused to a due sense of their responsibility in this matter, he will feel that his book has not been written in vain.'

Gilbert (Dr. G. H.)—A PRIMER OF THE CHRISTIAN RELIGION.   Based on the Teaching of Jesus, its Founder and Living Lord.   Crown 8vo.   4s. 6d. net.

Palmer (Florence U.)—ONE YEAR OF SUNDAY SCHOOL LESSONS FOR YOUNG CHILDREN.   Adapted for use in the Youngest Classes.   Pott 4to.   4s. 6d.

Sermons, Lectures, Addresses, and Theological Essays

(See also 'Bible,' 'Church of England,' 'Fathers')

Abbey (Rev. C. J.)—THE DIVINE LOVE : ITS STERN-NESS, BREADTH, AND TENDERNESS.   Crown 8vo.   6s.

GUARDIAN.—"This is a book which, in our opinion, demands the most serious and earnest attention."

Abbott (Rev. E. A.)—

CAMBRIDGE SERMONS. 8vo. 6s.

OXFORD SERMONS. 8vo. 7s. 6d.

PHILOMYTHUS. An Antidote against Credulity. A discussion of Cardinal Newman's Essay on Ecclesiastical Miracles. 2nd Edition. Crown 8vo. 3s. 6d.

THE SPIRIT ON THE WATERS, OR DIVINE EVOLUTION AS THE BASIS OF CHRISTIAN BELIEF. 8vo. 12s. 6d. net.

Abrahams (I.)—**Montefiore** (C. G.)—ASPECTS OF JUDAISM. Being Sixteen Sermons. 2nd Edition. Fcap. 8vo. 3s. 6d. net.

TIMES.—"There is a great deal in them that does not appeal to Jews alone, for, especially in Mr. Montefiore's addresses, the doctrines advocated, with much charm of style, are often not by any means exclusively Jewish, but such as are shared and honoured by all who care for religion and morality as those terms are commonly understood in the western world."

GLASGOW HERALD.—"Both from the homiletic and what may be called the big-world point of view, this little volume is one of considerable interest."

Ainger (Rev. Alfred, Master of the Temple). — SERMONS PREACHED IN THE TEMPLE CHURCH. Extra fcap. 8vo. 6s.

Askwith (E. H.)—THE CHRISTIAN CONCEPTION OF HOLINESS. Crown 8vo. 6s.

THE SPECTATOR.—"A well-reasoned and really noble view of the essential purpose of the Christian revelation. . . . We hope that Mr. Askwith's work will be widely read."

Bather (Archdeacon).—ON SOME MINISTERIAL DUTIES, CATECHISING, PREACHING, ETC. Edited, with a Preface, by Very Rev. C. J. VAUGHAN, D.D. Fcap. 8vo. 4s. 6d.

Beeching (Rev. Canon H. C.)—INNS OF COURT SERMONS. Crown 8vo. 4s. 6d.

Benson (Archbishop)—

BOY-LIFE: its Trial, its Strength, its Fulness. Sundays in Wellington College, 1859-73. 4th Edition. Crown 8vo. 6s.

CHRIST AND HIS TIMES. Addressed to the Diocese of Canterbury in his Second Visitation. Crown 8vo. 6s.

FISHERS OF MEN. Addressed to the Diocese of Canterbury in his Third Visitation. Crown 8vo. 6s.

GUARDIAN.—"There is plenty of plain speaking in the addresses before us, and they contain many wise and thoughtful counsels on subjects of the day."

TIMES.—"With keen insight and sagacious counsel, the Archbishop surveys the condition and prospects of the church."

ARCHBISHOP BENSON IN IRELAND. A record of his Irish Sermons and Addresses. Edited by J. H. BERNARD. Crown 8vo. 3s. 6d.

PALL MALL GAZETTE.—"No words of mine could appreciate, or do justice to, the stately language and lofty thoughts of the late Primate; they will appeal to every Churchman."

Bernard (Canon T.D.).—THE SONGS OF THE HOLY NATIVITY CONSIDERED (1) AS RECORDED IN SCRIPTURE, (2) AS IN USE IN THE CHURCH. Crown 8vo. 5s.

To use the words of its author, this book is offered "to readers of Scripture as expository of a distinct portion of the Holy Word; to worshippers in the congregation as a devotional commentary on the hymns which they use; to those keeping Christmas, as a contribution to the ever-welcome thoughts of that blessed season; to all Christian people who, in the midst of the historical elaboration of Christianity, find it good to re-enter from time to time the clear atmosphere of its origin, and are fain in the heat of the day to recover some feeling of the freshness of dawn."

GLASGOW HERALD.—"He conveys much useful information in a scholarly way."
SCOTSMAN.—"Their meaning and their relationships, the reasons why the Church has adopted them, and many other kindred points, are touched upon in the book with so well-explained a learning and with so much insight that the book will be highly valued by those interested in its subject."

Brooke (Rev. Stopford A.)—SHORT SERMONS. Cr. 8vo. 6s.

Brooks (Phillips, late Bishop of Massachusetts)—

THE CANDLE OF THE LORD, and other Sermons. Crown 8vo. 6s.

SERMONS PREACHED IN ENGLISH CHURCHES. Crown 8vo. 6s.

TWENTY SERMONS. Crown 8vo. 6s.

THE LIGHT OF THE WORLD. Crown 8vo. 3s. 6d.

THE MYSTERY OF INIQUITY. Crown 8vo. 6s.

ESSAYS AND ADDRESSES, RELIGIOUS, LITERARY, AND SOCIAL. Edited by the Rev. JOHN COTTON BROOKS. Crown 8vo. 8s. 6d. net.

NEW STARTS IN LIFE, AND OTHER SERMONS. Crown 8vo. 6s.

WESTMINSTER GAZETTE.—"All characterised by that fervent piety, catholicity of spirit, and fine command of language for which the Bishop was famous."

THE MORE ABUNDANT LIFE. Lenten Readings. Royal 16mo. 5s.

THE LAW OF GROWTH, and other Sermons. Crown 8vo. 6s.

SCOTSMAN.—"All instinct with the piety, breadth of mind, and eloquence which have given Phillips Brooks' pulpit prolocutions their rare distinction among productions of this kind, that of being really and truly suitable for more Sundays than one."
GLOBE.—"So manly in outlook and so fresh and suggestive in treatment."

THE INFLUENCE OF JESUS. The Bohlen Lectures, 1879. Crown 8vo. 6s.

LECTURES ON PREACHING DELIVERED AT YALE COLLEGE. Crown 8vo. 6s.

LIFE AND LETTERS OF PHILLIPS BROOKS. By A. V. G. ALLEN. 3 vols. 8vo. 30s. net.

Brunton (Sir T. Lauder). — THE BIBLE AND SCIENCE. With Illustrations. Crown 8vo. 10s. 6d.

Campbell (Dr. John M'Leod)—

THE NATURE OF THE ATONEMENT. 6th Ed. Cr. 8vo. 6s.

Campbell (Dr. John M'Leod)—*continued.*

THOUGHTS ON REVELATION. 2nd Edition. Crown 8vo. 5s.

RESPONSIBILITY FOR THE GIFT OF ETERNAL LIFE. Compiled from Sermons preached at Row, in the years 1829-31. Crown 8vo. 5s.

Carpenter (W. Boyd, Bishop of Ripon)—

TRUTH IN TALE. Addresses, chiefly to Children. Crown 8vo. 4s. 6d.

THE PERMANENT ELEMENTS OF RELIGION : Bampton Lectures, 1887. 2nd Edition. Crown 8vo. 6s.

TWILIGHT DREAMS. Crown 8vo. 4s. 6d.

LECTURES ON PREACHING. Crown 8vo. 3s. 6d. net.

TIMES.—" These *Lectures on Preaching,* delivered a year ago in the Divinity School at Cambridge, are an admirable analysis of the intellectual, ethical, spiritual, and rhetorical characteristics of the art of preaching. In six lectures the Bishop deals successfully with the preacher and his training, with the sermon and its structure, with the preacher and his age, and with the aim of the preacher. In each case he is practical, suggestive, eminently stimulating, and often eloquent, not with the mere splendour of rhetoric, but with the happy faculty of saying the right thing in well-chosen words."

SOME THOUGHTS ON CHRISTIAN REUNION. Being a Charge to the Clergy. Crown 8vo. 3s. 6d. net.

TIMES.—" Dr. Boyd Carpenter treats this very difficult subject with moderation and good sense, and with a clear-headed perception of the limits which inexorably circumscribe the natural aspirations of Christians of different churches and nationalities for a more intimate communion and fellowship."

LEEDS MERCURY.—" He discusses with characteristic vigour and felicity the claims which hinder reunion, and the true idea and scope of catholicity."

Chase (Rev. Dr. F. H.).—THE SUPERNATURAL ELEMENT IN OUR LORD'S EARTHLY LIFE IN RELATION TO HISTORICAL METHODS OF STUDY. 8vo. Sewed. 1s.

Cheetham (Archdeacon). — MYSTERIES, PAGAN AND CHRISTIAN. Being the Hulsean Lectures for 1896. Crown 8vo. 5s.

Church (Dean)—

HUMAN LIFE AND ITS CONDITIONS. Crown 8vo. 6s.

THE GIFTS OF CIVILISATION, and other Sermons and Lectures. 2nd Edition. Crown 8vo. 7s. 6d.

DISCIPLINE OF THE CHRISTIAN CHARACTER, and other Sermons. Crown 8vo. 4s. 6d.

ADVENT SERMONS. 1885. Crown 8vo. 4s. 6d.

VILLAGE SERMONS. Crown 8vo. 6s.

VILLAGE SERMONS. Second Series. Crown 8vo. 6s.

VILLAGE SERMONS. Third Series. Crown 8vo. 6s.

TIMES.—" In these sermons we see how a singularly gifted and cultivated mind was able to communicate its thoughts on the highest subjects to those with whom it might be supposed to have little in common. . . . His village sermons are not the by-work, if one whose interests were elsewhere in higher matters. They are the outcome of his deepest interests and of the life of his choice. . . . These sermons are worth perusal if only to show what preaching, even to the humble and unlearned hearers, may be made in really competent hands."

Church (Dean)—*continued.*

CATHEDRAL AND UNIVERSITY SERMONS. Crown 8vo. 6s.

PASCAL AND OTHER SERMONS. Crown 8vo. 6s.

TIMES.—"They are all eminently characteristic of one of the most saintly of modern divines, and one of the most scholarly of modern men of letters."

SPECTATOR.—"Dean Church's seem to us the finest sermons published since Newman's, even Dr. Liddon's rich and eloquent discourses not excepted,—and they breathe more of the spirit of perfect peace than even Newman's. They cannot be called High Church or Broad Church, much less Low Church sermons; they are simply the sermons of a good scholar, a great thinker, and a firm and serene Christian."

CLERGYMAN'S SELF-EXAMINATION CONCERNING THE APOSTLES' CREED. Extra fcap. 8vo. 1s. 6d.

Congreve (Rev. John).—HIGH HOPES AND PLEADINGS FOR A REASONABLE FAITH, NOBLER THOUGHTS, LARGER CHARITY. Crown 8vo. 5s.

Davidson (Archbishop)—

A CHARGE DELIVERED TO THE CLERGY OF THE DIOCESE OF ROCHESTER, October 29, 30, 31, 1894. 8vo. Sewed. 2s. net.

A CHARGE DELIVERED TO THE CLERGY OF THE DIOCESE OF WINCHESTER, Sept. 28, 30, Oct. 2, 3, 4, and 5, 1899. 8vo. Sewed. 2s. 6d. net.

Davies (Rev. J. Llewelyn)—

THE GOSPEL AND MODERN LIFE. 2nd Edition, to which is added Morality according to the Sacrament of the Lord's Supper. Extra fcap. 8vo. 6s.

SOCIAL QUESTIONS FROM THE POINT OF VIEW OF CHRISTIAN THEOLOGY. 2nd Edition. Crown 8vo. 6..

WARNINGS AGAINST SUPERSTITION. Extra fcap. 8vo. 2s. 6d.

THE CHRISTIAN CALLING. Extra fcap. 8vo. 6s.

BAPTISM, CONFIRMATION, AND THE LORD'S SUPPER, as interpreted by their Outward Signs. Three Addresses. New Edition. Pott 8vo. 1s.

ORDER AND GROWTH AS INVOLVED IN THE SPIRITUAL CONSTITUTION OF HUMAN SOCIETY. Crown 8vo. 3s. 6d.

GLASGOW HERALD.—"This is a wise and suggestive book, touching upon many of the more interesting questions of the present day. . . . A book as full of hope as it is of ability."

MANCHESTER GUARDIAN.—"He says what he means, but never more than he means; and hence his words carry weight with many to whom the ordinary sermon would appeal in vain. . . . The whole book is well worth study."

ABERDEEN DAILY FREE PRESS.—"An able discussion of the true basis and aim of social progress."

SCOTSMAN.—"Thoughtful and suggestive."

Davies (Rev. J. Llewelyn)—*continued.*

SPIRITUAL APPREHENSION : Sermons and Papers.   Crown
8vo. 6s.

Davies (W.) — THE PILGRIM OF THE INFINITE.   A
Discourse addressed to Advanced Religious Thinkers on Christian
Lines.   By WM. DAVIES. Fcap. 8vo. 3s. 6d.

CHRISTIAN WORLD.—"We hail this work as one which in an age of much
mental unrest sounds a note of faith which appeals confidently to the highest intellect,
inasmuch as it springs out of the clearest intuitions of the human spirit."

Ellerton (Rev. John). — THE HOLIEST MANHOOD, AND
ITS LESSONS FOR BUSY LIVES. Crown 8vo. 6s.

English Theological Library.   Edited by Rev. FREDERIC
RELTON.   With General Introduction by the late BISHOP
CREIGHTON.   A Series of Texts Annotated for the Use of
Students, Candidates for Ordination, etc.   8vo.

Re-issue at Reduced Prices.

I. HOOKER'S ECCLESIASTICAL POLITY, Book V., Edited
by Rev. Ronald E. Bayne. 10s. 6d. net.

II. LAW'S SERIOUS CALL, Edited by Rev. Canon J. H. Overton.
4s. 6d. net.

DAILY NEWS.—"A well-executed reprint. . . . Canon Overton's notes are not
numerous, and are as a rule very interesting and useful."
CAMBRIDGE REVIEW.—"A welcome reprint. . . . All that it should be in
paper and appearance, and the reputation of the editor is a guarantee for the accuracy
and fairness of the notes."

III. WILSON'S MAXIMS, Edited by Rev. F. Relton. 3s. 6d. net.

GUARDIAN.—"Many readers will feel grateful to Mr. Relton for this edition of
Bishop Wilson's ' Maxims.' . . . Mr. Relton's edition will be found well worth possessing : it is pleasant to the eye, and bears legible marks of industry and study."
EXPOSITORY TIMES.—"In an introduction of some twenty pages, he tells us
all we need to know of Bishop Wilson and of his maxims. Then he gives us the maxims
themselves in most perfect form, and schools himself to add at the bottom of the page
such notes as are absolutely necessary to their understanding, and nothing more."

IV. THE WORKS OF BISHOP BUTLER. Vol. I. Sermons,
Charges, Fragments, and Correspondence. Vol. II. The Analogy
of Religion, and two brief dissertations : I. Of Personal Identity.
II. Of the Nature of Virtue. Edited by the Very Rev. J. H.
BERNARD, D.D., Dean of St. Patrick's, Dublin. 4s. 6d. net each.

THE PILOT.—"One could hardly desire a better working edition than this which
Dr. Bernard has given us. . . . Sure to become the standard edition for students."
THE SPECTATOR.—"An excellent piece of work."

V. THE CONFERENCE BETWEEN WILLIAM LAUD AND
MR. FISHER, THE JESUIT. Edited by Rev. C. H. SIMP-
KINSON, M.A. Author of *The Life of Archbishop Laud.*

[4s. 6d. net.

Everett (Dr. C. C.)—THE PSYCHOLOGICAL ELEMENTS
OF RELIGIOUS FAITH. Crown 8vo. 5s. net.

EVIL AND EVOLUTION. An attempt to turn the Light of Modern
Science on to the Ancient Mystery of Evil. By the author of
The Social Horizon. Crown 8vo. 3s. 6d. net.

EXPOSITORY TIMES.—"The book is well worth the interest it is almost certain
to excite."

CHURCH TIMES.—"There can be no question about the courage or the keen
logic and the lucid style of this fascinating treatment of a problem which is of pathetic
interest to all of us. . . . It deserves to be studied by all, and no one who reads it can
fail to be struck by it."

FAITH AND CONDUCT: An Essay on Verifiable Religion. Crown
8vo. 7s. 6d.

Farrar (Very Rev. F. W., Dean of Canterbury)—

THE HISTORY OF INTERPRETATION. Being the Bampton
Lectures, 1885. 8vo. 16s.

Collected Edition of the Sermons, etc. Cr. 8vo. 3s. 6d. each.

SEEKERS AFTER GOD.
ETERNAL HOPE. Sermons Preached in Westminster Abbey.
THE FALL OF MAN, and other Sermons.
THE WITNESS OF HISTORY TO CHRIST. Hulsean Lectures.
THE SILENCE AND VOICES OF GOD.
IN THE DAYS OF THY YOUTH. Sermons on Practical Subjects.
SAINTLY WORKERS. Five Lenten Lectures.
EPHPHATHA: or, The Amelioration of the World.
MERCY AND JUDGMENT. A few words on Christian Eschatology.
SERMONS AND ADDRESSES delivered in America.

Fiske (John).—MAN'S DESTINY VIEWED IN THE LIGHT
OF HIS ORIGIN. Crown 8vo. 3s. 6d.

LIFE EVERLASTING. Globe 8vo. 3s. 6d.

Foxell (W. J.)—GOD'S GARDEN: Sunday Talks with Boys.
With an Introduction by Dean FARRAR. Globe 8vo. 3s. 6d.

SPEAKER.—"Deals with obvious problems of faith and conduct in a strain of
vigorous simplicity, and with an evident knowledge of the needs, the moods, the difficulties of boy-life. It is the kind of book which instils lessons of courage, trust, patience,
and forbearance; and does so quite as much by example as by precept."

IN A PLAIN PATH. Addresses to Boys. Globe 8vo. 3s. 6d.

SPEAKER.—"He handles with admirable vigour, and real discernment of a boy's
difficulties, such high themes as the use of time, noble revenge, the true gentleman, the
noblest victory, and progress through failure. There is nothing childish in the method of
treatment, and yet we feel sure that a man who spoke to a congregation of lads in this
fashion would not talk over the head of the youngest, and yet find his way to the hearts
of those who are just passing from the restraints of school to the responsibilities of life."

Fraser (Bishop).—UNIVERSITY SERMONS. Edited by
Rev. JOHN W. DIGGLE. Crown 8vo. 6s.

Goodspeed (G. S.)—ISRAEL'S MESSIANIC HOPE TO THE
TIME OF JESUS: A Study in the Historical Development of
the Foreshadowings of the Christ in the Old Testament and
beyond. Crown 8vo. 6s.

Grane (W. L.)—THE WORD AND THE WAY: or, The Light of the Ages on the Path of To-Day. Crown 8vo. 6s.

HARD SAYINGS OF JESUS CHRIST. A Study in the Mind and Method of the Master. Second Edition. Crown 8vo. 5s.

Green (S. G.)—THE CHRISTIAN CREED AND THE CREEDS OF CHRISTENDOM. Seven Lectures delivered in 1898 at Regent's Park College. Crown 8vo. 6s.

Harcourt (Sir W. V.)—LAWLESSNESS IN THE NATIONAL CHURCH. 8vo. Sewed. 1s. net.

Hardwick (Archdeacon). — CHRIST AND OTHER MASTERS. 6th Edition. Crown 8vo. 10s. 6d.

Hare (Julius Charles).—THE MISSION OF THE COMFORTER. New Edition. Edited by Dean PLUMPTRE. Crown 8vo. 7s. 6d.

Harris (Rev. G. C.) — SERMONS. With a Memoir by CHARLOTTE M. YONGE, and Portrait. Extra fcap. 8vo. 6s.

Henson (Canon H. H.)—SERMON ON THE DEATH OF THE QUEEN. 8vo. Sewed. 1s. net.

Hicks (Rev. Canon E. L.)—ADDRESSES ON THE TEMPTATION OF OUR LORD. Crown 8vo.   [*In the Press.*]

Hillis (N. D.) — THE INFLUENCE OF CHRIST IN MODERN LIFE. A Study of the New Problems of the Church in American Society. Crown 8vo. 6s.

THE QUEST OF HAPPINESS. A Study of Victory over Life's Troubles. Extra crown 8vo. 6s. net.

Hodgkins (Louise M.)—VIA CHRISTI : An Introduction to the Study of Missions. Globe 8vo. 2s. net. Sewed. 1s. 3d. net.

Hort (Dr. F. J. A.)—THE WAY, THE TRUTH, THE LIFE. Hulsean Lectures, 1871. Crown 8vo. 6s.

CAMBRIDGE REVIEW.—" Only to few is it given to scan the wide fields of truth with clear vision of near and far alike. To what an extraordinary degree the late Dr. Hort possessed this power is shown by the Hulsean Lectures just published. They carry us in the most wonderful way to the very centre of the Christian system ; no aspect of truth, no part of the world, seems to be left out of view ; while in every page we recognise the gathered fruits of a rare scholarship in the service of an unwearying thought."

JUDAISTIC CHRISTIANITY. Crown 8vo. 6s.

SCOTSMAN.—"The great merit of Dr. Hort's lectures is that succinctly and yet fully, and in a clear and interesting and suggestive manner, they give us not only his own opinions, but whatever of worth has been advanced on the subject."

GLASGOW HERALD.—"Will receive a respectful welcome at the hands of all biblical scholars. . . . A model of exact and patient scholarship, controlled by robust English sagacity, and it is safe to say that it will take a high place in the literature of the subject."

VILLAGE SERMONS. Crown 8vo. 6s.

Selected from the Sermons preached by Professor HORT to his village congregation at St. Ippolyt's, and including a series of Sermons dealing in a broad and suggestive way with the successive books of the Bible, from Genesis to Revelations.

Hort (Dr. F. J. A.)—*continued.*

SERMONS ON THE BOOKS OF THE BIBLE (selected from *Village Sermons*). Crown 8vo. 3s. 6d.

VILLAGE SERMONS IN OUTLINE. Crown 8vo. 6s.

      CONTENTS : I. The Prayer Book, 16 Sermons. II. Baptism, 5 Sermons. III. Mutual Subjection the Rule of Life (Eph. v. 21), 6 Sermons. IV. The Sermon on the Mount (St. Matt. v. 1 ; vii. 29), 11 Sermons. V. Advent, 4 Sermons. VI. The Armour of the Cross. VII. The Resurrection, 7 Sermons.

CAMBRIDGE AND OTHER SERMONS. Crown 8vo. 6s.

Hughes (T.)—THE MANLINESS OF CHRIST. 2nd Ed. Fcap. 8vo. 3s. 6d.

GLOBE.—"*The Manliness of Christ* is a species of lay sermon such as Judge Hughes is well qualified to deliver, seeing that manliness of thought and feeling has been the prevailing characteristic of all his literary products."
BRITISH WEEKLY.—"A new edition of a strong book."

Hutton (R. H.)—

ESSAYS ON SOME OF THE MODERN GUIDES OF ENG-LISH THOUGHT IN MATTERS OF FAITH. Globe 8vo. 4s. net.

THEOLOGICAL ESSAYS. Globe 8vo. 4s. net.

ASPECTS OF RELIGIOUS AND SCIENTIFIC THOUGHT. Selected from the *Spectator*, and edited by E. M. ROSCOE. Globe 8vo. 4s. net.

Hyde (W. DE W.)—OUTLINES OF SOCIAL THEOLOGY. Crown 8vo. 6s.

    Dr. Hyde thus describes the object of his book : " This little book aims to point out the logical relations in which the doctrines of theology will stand to each other when the time shall come again for seeing Christian truth in the light of reason and Christian life as the embodiment of love."

PRACTICAL IDEALISM. Globe 8vo. 5s. net.

Illingworth (Rev. J. R.)—SERMONS PREACHED IN A COLLEGE CHAPEL. Crown 8vo. 5s.

UNIVERSITY AND CATHEDRAL SERMONS. Crown 8vo. 5s.

PERSONALITY, DIVINE AND HUMAN. Bampton Lectures, 1894. Crown 8vo. 6s.

TIMES.—"Will take high rank among the rare theological masterpieces produced by that celebrated foundation."
EXPOSITOR.—"It is difficult to convey an adequate impression of the freshness and strength of the whole argument. . . . It is a book which no one can be satisfied with reading once ; it is to be studied."

DIVINE IMMANENCE. An Essay on the Spiritual Significance of Matter. New Edition. Cr. 8vo. 6s.

CHURCH QUARTERLY REVIEW.—"A very valuable book. . . . *Divine Immanence* is likely to prove of great service to Christian truth. It combines, to a remarkable extent, profound thought and clear expression. It is throughout written in an interesting style."
GUARDIAN.—"Altogether, we have rarely read a book of such philosophical earnestness in construing the Christian view of existence in terms of the thought and knowledge of these days, nor one more likely to bring home the knowledge of a Saviour to the modern man."

Illingworth (Rev. J. R.)—*continued.*

    REASON AND REVELATION. An Essay in Christian Apology. 8vo. 7s. 6d.

Jacob (Rev. J. A.) — BUILDING IN SILENCE, and other Sermons. Extra fcap. 8vo. 6s.

Jacob (Rev. J. T.).—CHRIST THE INDWELLER. Cr. 8vo. 5s.

Jellett (Rev. Dr.)—

    THE ELDER SON, and other Sermons. Crown 8vo. 6s.

Joceline (E.)—THE MOTHER'S LEGACIE TO HER UN-BORN CHILD. Cr. 16mo. 4s. 6d.

Jones (Jenkin Lloyd)—

    JESS : BITS OF WAYSIDE GOSPEL. Crown 8vo. 6s.

    A SEARCH FOR AN INFIDEL : BITS OF WAYSIDE GOS-PEL. Second Series. Crown 8vo. 6s.

Kellogg (Rev. S. H.)—

    THE GENESIS AND GROWTH OF RELIGION. Cr. 8vo. 6s.

    SCOTSMAN.—" Full of matter of an important kind, set forth with praiseworthy conciseness, and at the same time with admirable lucidity. . . . Dr. Kellogg has done the work allotted to him with great ability, and everywhere manifests a competent acquaintance with the subject with which he deals."

King (Prof. H. C.)—RECONSTRUCTION IN THEOLOGY. Crown 8vo. 6s.

    THEOLOGY AND THE SOCIAL CONSCIOUSNESS. Crown 8vo. 5s. net.

Kingsley (Charles)—

    VILLAGE AND TOWN AND COUNTRY SERMONS. Crown 8vo. 3s. 6d.

    THE WATER OF LIFE, and other Sermons. Crown 8vo. 3s. 6d.

    SERMONS ON NATIONAL SUBJECTS, AND THE KING OF THE EARTH. Crown 8vo. 3s. 6d.

    SERMONS FOR THE TIMES. Crown 8vo. 3s. 6d.

    GOOD NEWS OF GOD. Crown 8vo. 3s. 6d.

    THE GOSPEL OF THE PENTATEUCH, AND DAVID. Crown 8vo. 3s. 6d.

    DISCIPLINE, and other Sermons. Crown 8vo. 3s. 6d.

    WESTMINSTER SERMONS. Crown 8vo. 3s. 6d.

    ALL SAINTS' DAY, and other Sermons. Crown 8vo. 3s. 6d.

    ACADEMY.—" We can imagine nothing more appropriate than this edition for a public, a school, or even a village library."

Kirkpatrick (Prof. A. F.)—THE DIVINE LIBRARY OF THE OLD TESTAMENT. Its Origin, Preservation, Inspiration, and Permanent Value. Crown 8vo. 3s. net.

    THE DOCTRINE OF THE PROPHETS. Warburtonian Lectures 1886-1890. Third Edition. Crown 8vo. 6s.

Knight (W. A.)—ASPECTS OF THEISM. 8vo. 8s. 6d.

LETTERS FROM HELL. Newly translated from the Danish. With an Introduction by Dr. GEORGE MACDONALD. Twenty-eighth Thousand. Crown 8vo. 2s. 6d.

Lightfoot (Bishop)—

THE CHRISTIAN MINISTRY. Reprinted from *Dissertations on the Apostolic Age.* Crown 8vo. 3s. net.

LEADERS IN THE NORTHERN CHURCH : Sermons Preached in the Diocese of Durham. 2nd Edition. Crown 8vo. 6s.

ORDINATION ADDRESSES AND COUNSELS TO CLERGY. Crown 8vo. 6s.

CAMBRIDGE SERMONS. Crown 8vo. 6s.

SERMONS PREACHED IN ST. PAUL'S CATHEDRAL. Crown 8vo. 6s.

SERMONS PREACHED ON SPECIAL OCCASIONS. Crown 8vo. 6s.

A CHARGE DELIVERED TO THE CLERGY OF THE DIOCESE OF DURHAM, 25th Nov. 1886. Demy 8vo. 2s.

ESSAYS ON THE WORK ENTITLED "Supernatural Religion." 8vo. Re-issue at 6s. net.

DISSERTATIONS ON THE APOSTOLIC AGE. 8vo. 14s.

BIBLICAL ESSAYS. 8vo. 12s.

TIMES.—"As representing all that is now available of the Bishop's profound learning and consummate scholarship for the illustration of his great subject, the present volume and its successor will be warmly welcomed by all students of theology."

Lillingston (Frank, M.A.)—THE BRAMO SAMAJ AND ARYA SAMAJ IN THEIR BEARING UPON CHRISTIANITY. A Study in Indian Theism. Cr. 8vo. 2s. 6d. net.

Macmillan (Rev. Hugh)—

BIBLE TEACHINGS IN NATURE. 15th Ed. Globe 8vo. 6s.

THE TRUE VINE ; OR, THE ANALOGIES OF OUR LORD'S ALLEGORY. 5th Edition. Globe 8vo. 6s.

THE MINISTRY OF NATURE. 8th Edition. Globe 8vo. 6s.

THE SABBATH OF THE FIELDS. 6th Edition. Globe 8vo. 6s.

THE MARRIAGE IN CANA. Globe 8vo. 6s.

TWO WORLDS ARE OURS. 3rd Edition. Globe 8vo. 6s.

THE OLIVE LEAF. Globe 8vo. 6s.

THE GATE BEAUTIFUL AND OTHER BIBLE TEACHINGS FOR THE YOUNG. Crown 8vo. 3s. 6d.

SPEAKER.—"These addresses are, in fact, models of their kind—wise, reverent, and not less imaginative than practical ; they abound in choice and apposite anecdotes and illustrations, and possess distinct literary merit."

DAILY CHRONICLE.—"The poetic touch that beautifies all Dr. Macmillan's writing is fresh in every one of these charming addresses. The volume is sure to meet with cordial appreciation far beyond the sphere of its origin."

GLEANINGS IN HOLY FIELDS. Crown 8vo. 3s. 6d.

THE CORN OF HEAVEN. Crown 8vo. 6s.

Mahaffy (Rev. Prof.)—THE DECAY OF MODERN PREACHING : AN ESSAY. Crown 8vo. 3s. 6d.

Marshall (H. Rutgers)—INSTINCT AND REASON: An Essay with some Special Study of the Nature of Religion. 8vo. 12s. 6d. net.

Mason (Caroline A.)—LUX CHRISTI. An Outline Study of India—A Twilight Land. Crown 8vo. 2s. net.

Mathews (S.).—THE SOCIAL TEACHING OF JESUS: AN ESSAY IN CHRISTIAN SOCIOLOGY. Crown 8vo. 6s.

Maurice (Frederick Denison)—

THE KINGDOM OF CHRIST. 3rd Ed. 2 Vols. Cr. 8vo. 7s.

THE CONSCIENCE. Lectures on Casuistry. 3rd Ed. Cr. 8vo. 4s. 6d.

DIALOGUES ON FAMILY WORSHIP. Crown 8vo. 4s. 6d.

THE DOCTRINE OF SACRIFICE DEDUCED FROM THE SCRIPTURES. 2nd Edition. Crown 8vo. 6s.

THE RELIGIONS OF THE WORLD. 6th Edition. Cr. 8vo. 4s. 6d.

ON THE SABBATH DAY; THE CHARACTER OF THE WARRIOR; AND ON THE INTERPRETATION OF HISTORY. Fcap. 8vo. 2s. 6d.

LEARNING AND WORKING. Crown 8vo. 4s. 6d.

THE LORD'S PRAYER, THE CREED, AND THE COMMANDMENTS. Pott 8vo. 1s.

Collected Works. Crown 8vo. 3s. 6d. each.

SERMONS PREACHED IN LINCOLN'S INN CHAPEL. In Six Volumes. 3s. 6d. each.

CHRISTMAS DAY AND OTHER SERMONS.

THEOLOGICAL ESSAYS.

PROPHETS AND KINGS.

PATRIARCHS AND LAWGIVERS.

THE GOSPEL OF THE KINGDOM OF HEAVEN.

GOSPEL OF ST. JOHN.

EPISTLE OF ST. JOHN.

FRIENDSHIP OF BOOKS.

PRAYER BOOK AND LORD'S PRAYER.

THE DOCTRINE OF SACRIFICE.

THE ACTS OF THE APOSTLES.

CHURCH TIMES.—"There is probably no writer of the present century to whom the English Church owes a deeper debt of gratitude. . . . Probably he did more to stop the stream of converts to Romanism which followed the secession of Newman than any other individual, by teaching English Churchmen to think out the reasonableness of their position."

SPEAKER.—"These sermons are marked in a conspicuous degree by high thinking and plain statement."

TIMES.—"A volume of sermons for which the memory of Maurice's unique personal influence ought to secure a cordial reception."

SCOTSMAN.—"They appear in a volume uniform with the recent collective edition of Maurice's works, and will be welcome to the many readers to whom that edition has brought home the teaching of the most popular among modern English divines."

Medley (Rev. W.)—CHRIST THE TRUTH. Being the
Angus Lectures for the year 1900. Crown 8vo. 6s.

Milligan (Rev. Prof. W.)—THE RESURRECTION OF OUR
LORD. Fourth Edition. Crown 8vo. 5s.

SPECTATOR.—"The argument is put with brevity and force by Dr. Milligan, and
every page bears witness that he has mastered the literature of the subject, and has made
a special study of the more recent discussions on this aspect of the question. . . . The
remaining lectures are more theological. They abound in striking views, in fresh and
vigorous exegesis, and manifest a keen apprehension of the bearing of the fact of the
Resurrection on many important questions of theology. The notes are able and
scholarly, and elucidate the teaching of the text."

THE ASCENSION AND HEAVENLY PRIESTHOOD OF
OUR LORD. *Baird Lectures,* 1891. Crown 8vo. 7s. 6d.

Montefiore (Claude G.)—LIBERAL JUDAISM. An Essay.
Crown 8vo. 3s. net.

Moorhouse (Bishop)—

JACOB : Three Sermons. Extra fcap. 8vo. 3s. 6d.
THE TEACHING OF CHRIST. Its Conditions, Secret, and
Results. Crown 8vo. 3s. net.
DANGERS OF THE APOSTOLIC AGE. Crown 8vo. 3s. net.
CHURCH WORK : ITS MEANS AND METHODS. Crown
8vo. 3s. net.

CHURCH TIMES.—"It may almost be said to mark an epoch, and to inaugurate a
new era in the history of Episcopal visitation."
TIMES.—"A series of diocesan addresses, full of practical counsel, by one of the
most active and sagacious of modern prelates."
GLOBE.—"Throughout the volume we note the presence of the wisdom that comes
from long and varied experience, from sympathy, and from the possession of a fair and
tolerant mind."
MANCHESTER GUARDIAN.—"Full of interest and instruction for all who take
an interest in social and moral, to say nothing of ecclesiastical, reforms, and deserves to
find careful students far beyond the limits of those to whom it was originally addressed."

Myers (F. W. H.)—SCIENCE AND A FUTURE LIFE.
Gl. 8vo. 4s. net.

Nash (H. S.)—GENESIS OF THE SOCIAL CONSCIENCE.
THE RELATION BETWEEN THE ESTABLISHMENT
OF CHRISTIANITY IN EUROPE AND THE SOCIAL
QUESTION. Crown 8vo. 6s.

SCOTSMAN.—"The book is eloquently, and at times brilliantly, written. . . . But
few readers could go through it without being inspired by its clever and animated hand-
ling of philosophical ideas."
MANCHESTER GUARDIAN.—"An interesting and suggestive little book."

Pattison (Mark).—SERMONS. Crown 8vo. 6s.

Peabody (Prof. F. G.)—JESUS CHRIST AND THE SOCIAL
QUESTION. Crown 8vo. 6s.

PEPLOGRAPHIA DVBLINENSIS. Memorial Discourses Preached
in the Chapel of Trinity College, Dublin, 1895-1902. With
Preface by the Very Rev. J. H. BERNARD, D.D., Dean of St.
Patrick's. Crown 8vo. 3s. 6d. net.

PHILOCHRISTUS. Memoirs of a Disciple of the Lord. 3rd Ed. 8vo. 12s.

Pike (G. R.)—THE DIVINE DRAMA THE DIVINE MANIFESTATION OF GOD IN THE UNIVERSE. Crown 8vo. 6s.

Plumptre (Dean). — MOVEMENTS IN RELIGIOUS THOUGHT. Fcap. 8vo. 3s. 6d.

PRO CHRISTO ET ECCLESIA. Second Impression. Crown 8vo. Gilt top. 4s. 6d. net.

BOOKMAN.—"It is not only its anonymity which suggests comparison with *Ecce Homo.* The subject is the same in both books—the method and aim of Jesus—though treated from quite different points of view ; and the level of thought is much the same ; the easy originality that cuts a new section through the life of Christ and shows us strata before unthought of ; the classic severity of the style, the penetrating knowledge of human nature, the catholicity of treatment, all remind us of Professor Seeley's captivating work."

Purchas (Rev. H. T.)—JOHANNINE PROBLEMS AND MODERN NEEDS. Crown 8vo. 3s. net.

Rendall (Rev. F.)—THE THEOLOGY OF THE HEBREW CHRISTIANS. Crown 8vo. 5s.

Ridding (George, Bishop of Southwell).—THE REVEL AND THE BATTLE. Crown 8vo. 6s.

TIMES.—"Singularly well worth reading."
MANCHESTER GUARDIAN.—"Marked by dignity and force."

Robinson (Prebendary H. G.)—MAN IN THE IMAGE OF GOD, and other Sermons. Crown 8vo. 7s. 6d.

Robinson (Dean J. A.)—UNITY IN CHRIST AND OTHER SERMONS. Crown 8vo. 6s.

Rutherford (Rev. Dr. W. G., Headmaster of Westminster).—THE KEY OF KNOWLEDGE. Sermons preached to Westminster Boys in the Abbey. Crown 8vo. 6s.

Seeley (Sir J. R.)—ECCE HOMO : A Survey of the Life and Work of Jesus Christ. Globe 8vo. 5s.

NATURAL RELIGION. Globe 8vo. 5s.

ATHENÆUM.—"If it be the function of a genius to interpret the age to itself, this is a work of genius. It gives articulate expression to the higher strivings of the time. It puts plainly the problem of these latter days, and so far contributes to its solution ; a positive solution it scarcely claims to supply. No such important contribution to the question of the time has been published in England since the appearance in 1866 of *Ecce Homo.* . . . The author is a teacher whose words it is well to listen to ; his words are wise but sad ; it has not been given him to fire them with faith, but only to light them with reason. His readers may at least thank him for the intellectual illumination, if they cannot owe him gratitude for any added favour. . . . A book which we assume will be read by most thinking Englishmen."
MANCHESTER GUARDIAN.—"The present issue is a compact, handy, well-printed edition of a thoughtful and remarkable book."

Selborne (Roundell, Earl of).—LETTERS TO HIS SON ON RELIGION. Globe 8vo. 3s. 6d.

THE CATHOLIC AND APOSTOLIC CHURCH. Globe 8vo. 3s. 6d.

Service (Rev. John).—SERMONS. With Portrait. Crown 8vo. 6s.

Stanley (Dean)—

THE NATIONAL THANKSGIVING. Sermons preached in Westminster Abbey. 2nd Edition. Crown 8vo. 2s. 6d.

Stewart (Prof. Balfour) and **Tait** (Prof. P. G.)—THE UNSEEN UNIVERSE; OR, PHYSICAL SPECULATIONS ON A FUTURE STATE. 15th Edition. Crown 8vo. 6s.

Stubbs (Dean)—

CHRISTUS IMPERATOR. A Series of Lecture-Sermons on the Universal Empire of Christianity. Edited by Very Rev. C. W. STUBBS, D.D., Dean of Ely. Crown 8vo. 6s.

The discourses included in this volume were delivered in 1893 in the Chapel-of-Ease to the Parish Church of Wavertree—at that time the centre of much excellent social work done by Mr. Stubbs, who had not yet been promoted to the Deanery of Ely. The following are the subjects and the preachers :—The Supremacy of Christ in all Realms : by the Very Rev. Charles Stubbs, D.D., Dean of Ely.—Christ in the Realm of History : by the Very Rev. G. W. Kitchin, D.D., Dean of Durham.—Christ in the Realm of Philosophy : by the Rev. R. E. Bartlett, M.A., Bampton Lecturer in 1888.—Christ in the Realm of Law : by the Rev. J. B. Heard, M.A., Hulsean Lecturer in 1893.—Christ in the Realm of Art : by the Rev. Canon Rawnsley, M.A., Vicar of Crosthwaite.—Christ in the Realm of Ethics : by the Rev. J. Llewelyn Davies, D.D., Vicar of Kirkby Lonsdale, and Chaplain to the Queen.—Christ in the Realm of Politics : by the Rev. and Hon. W. H. Freemantle, M.A., Canon of Canterbury.—Christ in the Realm of Science : by the Rev. Brooke Lambert, B.C.L., Vicar of Greenwich.—Christ in the Realm of Sociology : by the Rev. S. A. Barnett, M.A., Warden of Toynbee Hall, and Canon of Bristol.—Christ in the Realm of Poetry : by the Very Rev. Charles Stubbs, D.D., Dean of Ely.

SCOTSMAN.—"Their prelections will be found stimulating and instructive in a high degree. The volume deserves recognition as a courageous attempt to give to Christianity its rightful place and power in the lives of its professors."

Talbot (Bishop).—A CHARGE DELIVERED TO THE CLERGY OF THE DIOCESE OF ROCHESTER, October 24, 25, and 26, 1899. 8 o. Sewed. 2s. net.

Temple (Archbishop)—

SERMONS PREACHED IN THE CHAPEL OF RUGBY SCHOOL. Extra Fcap. 8vo. 4s. 6d.

SECOND SERIES. 3rd Ed. 6s.

THIRD SERIES. 4th Edition. 6s.

THE RELATIONS BETWEEN RELIGION AND SCIENCE. Bampton Lectures, 1884. New Impression, 1903. Cr. 8vo. 6s.

CHARGE DELIVERED AT HIS FIRST VISITATION. 8vo. Sewed. 1s. net.

(1) The Doctrine of the Eucharist ; (2) The Practice of Confession ; (3) Uniformity in Ceremonial ; (4) The Power of the Bishops.

FIVE OF THE LATEST UTTERANCES OF FREDERICK TEMPLE, ARCHBISHOP OF CANTERBURY. Crown 8vo. 1s. net.

Thackeray (H. St. John).—THE RELATION OF ST. PAUL TO CONTEMPORARY JEWISH THOUGHT. Crown 8vo. 6s.

Trench (Archbishop).—HULSEAN LECTURES. 8vo. 7s. 6d.

Vaughan (Dean)—

MEMORIALS OF HARROW SUNDAYS. 5th Edition. Crown 8vo. 10s. 6d.

HEROES OF FAITH. 2nd Edition. Crown 8vo. 6s.

LIFE'S WORK AND GOD'S DISCIPLINE. 3rd Edition. Extra fcap. 8vo. 2s. 6d.

THE WHOLESOME WORDS OF JESUS CHRIST. 2nd Edition. Fcap. 8vo. 3s. 6d.

FOES OF FAITH. 2nd Edition. Fcap. 8vo. 3s. 6d.

COUNSELS FOR YOUNG STUDENTS. Fcap. 8vo. 2s. 6d.

THE TWO GREAT TEMPTATIONS. 2nd Ed. Fcap. 8vo. 3s. 6d.

ADDRESSES FOR YOUNG CLERGYMEN. Extra fcap. 8vo. 4s. 6d.

"MY SON, GIVE ME THINE HEART." Extra fcap. 8vo. 5s.

TEMPLE SERMONS. Crown 8vo. 10s. 6d.

AUTHORISED OR REVISED? Sermons on some of the Texts in which the Revised Version differs from the Authorised. Crown 8vo. 7s. 6d.

LESSONS OF THE CROSS AND PASSION. WORDS FROM THE CROSS. THE REIGN OF SIN. THE LORD'S PRAYER. Four Courses of Lent Lectures. Crown 8vo. 10s. 6d.

UNIVERSITY SERMONS. NEW AND OLD. Cr. 8vo. 10s. 6d.

NOTES FOR LECTURES ON CONFIRMATION. Fcap. 8vo. 1s. 6d.

THE PRAYERS OF JESUS CHRIST : a closing volume of Lent Lectures delivered in the Temple Church. Globe 8vo. 3s. 6d.

DONCASTER SERMONS. Lessons of Life and Godliness, and Words from the Gospels. Cr. 8vo. 10s. 6d.

RESTFUL THOUGHTS IN RESTLESS TIMES. Cr. 8vo. 5s.

LAST WORDS IN THE TEMPLE CHURCH. Globe 8vo. 5s.

SATURDAY REVIEW.—"These discourses in thought, in style, have so much that is permanent and fine about them that they will stand the ordeal of being read by any serious man, even though he never heard Dr. Vaughan speak."

UNIVERSITY AND OTHER SERMONS. Crown 8vo. 6s.

TIMES.—"As specimens of pure and rhythmical English prose, rising here and there to flights of sober and chastened eloquence, yet withal breathing throughout an earnest and devotional spirit, these sermons would be hard to match."

SCOTSMAN.—"All are marked by the earnestness, scholarship, and strength of thought which invariably characterised the pulpit utterances of the preacher."

Vaughan (Rev. D. J.)—THE PRESENT TRIAL OF FAITH. Crown 8vo. 5s.

QUESTIONS OF THE DAY, SOCIAL, NATIONAL, AND RELIGIOUS. Crown 8vo. 5s.

NATIONAL OBSERVER.—"In discussing *Questions of the Day* Mr. D. J. Vaughan speaks with candour, ability, and common sense."

SCOTSMAN.—"They form an altogether admirable collection of vigorous and thoughtful pronouncements on a variety of social, national, and religious topics."

GLASGOW HERALD.—"A volume such as this is the best reply to those friends of the people who are for ever complaining that the clergy waste their time preaching antiquated dogma and personal salvation, and neglect the weightier matters of the law."

MANCHESTER GUARDIAN.—"He speaks boldly as well as thoughtfully, and what he has to say is always worthy of attention."

EXPOSITORY TIMES.—"Most of them are social, and these are the most interesting. And one feature of peculiar interest is that in those sermons which were preached twenty years ago Canon Vaughan saw the questions of to-day, and suggested the remedies we are beginning to apply."

Vaughan (Canon E. T.)—SOME REASONS OF OUR CHRISTIAN HOPE. Hulsean Lectures for 1875. Crown 8vo. 6s. 6d.

Venn (Dr. John).—ON SOME CHARACTERISTICS OF BELIEF, SCIENTIFIC AND RELIGIOUS. 8vo. 6s. 6d.

Welldon (Bishop).—THE SPIRITUAL LIFE, and other Sermons. Crown 8vo. 6s.

SCOTTISH LEADER.—"In a strain of quiet, persuasive eloquence, Bishop Welldon treats impressively of various aspects of the higher life. His discourses cannot fail both to enrich the heart and stimulate the mind of the earnest reader."

GLASGOW HERALD.—"They are cultured, reverent, and thoughtful productions."

THE REVELATION OF THE HOLY SPIRIT. Crown 8vo. 6s.

"I LIVE": BEING HINTS ON THE CHRISTIAN LIFE. Crown 8vo. 1s. 6d. net.

THE CONSECRATION OF THE STATE. An Essay. Crown 8vo. 2s. net.

Westcott (Bishop)—

ON THE RELIGIOUS OFFICE OF THE UNIVERSITIES. Sermons. Crown 8vo. 4s. 6d.

GIFTS FOR MINISTRY. Addresses to Candidates for Ordination. Crown 8vo. 1s. 6d.

THE VICTORY OF THE CROSS. Sermons preached during Holy Week, 1888, in Hereford Cathedral. Crown 8vo. 3s. 6d.

FROM STRENGTH TO STRENGTH. Three Sermons (In Memoriam J. B. D.) Crown 8vo. 2s.

THE REVELATION OF THE RISEN LORD. Cr. 8vo. 6s.

THE HISTORIC FAITH. 3rd Edition. Crown 8vo. 6s.

THE GOSPEL OF THE RESURRECTION. 6th Ed. Cr. 8vo. 6s.

THE REVELATION OF THE FATHER. Crown 8vo. 6s.

CHRISTUS CONSUMMATOR. 2nd Edition. Crown 8vo. 6s.

Westcott (Bishop)—*continued.*

SOME THOUGHTS FROM THE ORDINAL. Cr. 8vo.   1s. 6d.

SOCIAL ASPECTS OF CHRISTIANITY. Crown 8vo.   6s.

ESSAYS IN THE HISTORY OF RELIGIOUS THOUGHT IN THE WEST. Globe 8vo.   4s. net.

THE GOSPEL OF LIFE. Crown 8vo.   6s.

THE INCARNATION AND COMMON LIFE. Crown 8vo.   9s.

TIMES.—"A collection of sermons which possess, among other merits, the rare one of actuality, reflecting, as they frequently do, the Bishop's well-known and eager interest in social problems of the day."

CHRISTIAN ASPECTS OF LIFE. Crown 8vo.   7s. 6d.

CHURCH TIMES.—"We heartily commend this volume to the notice of our readers. . . . The Church of England is not likely to lose touch with the people of this country so long as she is guided by Bishops who show such a truly large-hearted sympathy with everything human as is here manifested by the present occupier of the see of Durham."

LITERATURE.—"A sermon of the national day of rest, and some attractive personal reminiscences of school days under James Prince Lee, are among the choicest parts of the volume, if we are to single out any portions from a work of dignified and valuable utterance."

DAILY NEWS.—"Through every page . . . runs the same enlightened sympathy with the living world. One forgets the Bishop in the Man, the Ecclesiastic in the Citizen, the Churchman in the Christian."

THE OBLIGATIONS OF EMPIRE. Cr. 8vo. Sewed.   3d. net.

LESSONS FROM WORK. CHARGES AND ADDRESSES. Second Impression. Crown 8vo.   6s.

ADDRESS DELIVERED TO MINERS, July 1901. Crown 8vo. Sewed.   6d.

WORDS OF FAITH AND HOPE. Crown 8vo.   4s. 6d.

White (A. D.)—A HISTORY OF THE WARFARE OF SCIENCE WITH THEOLOGY IN CHRISTENDOM. In Two Vols. 8vo.   21s. net.

TIMES.—"Is certainly one of the most comprehensive, and, in our judgment, one of the most valuable historical works that have appeared for many years. . . . He has chosen a large subject, but it is at least one which has clear and definite limits, and he has treated it very fully and comprehensively in two moderate volumes. . . . His book appears to us to be based on much original research, on an enormous amount of careful, accurate, and varied reading, and his habit of appending to each section a list of the chief books, both ancient and modern, relating to it will be very useful to serious students. He has decided opinions, but he always writes temperately, and with transparent truthfulness of intention."

DAILY CHRONICLE.—"The story of the struggle of searchers after truth with the organised forces of ignorance, bigotry, and superstition is the most inspiring chapter in the whole history of mankind. That story has never been better told than by the ex-President of Cornell University in these two volumes."

Wickham (Very Rev. Dean).—WELLINGTON COLLEGE SERMONS. Crown 8vo.   6s.

Wilkins (Prof. A. S.)—THE LIGHT OF THE WORLD : an Essay. 2nd Edition. Crown 8vo.   3s. 6d.

Wilson (Archdeacon)—

SERMONS PREACHED IN CLIFTON COLLEGE CHAPEL. Second Series. 1888-90. Crown 8vo.   6s.

Wilson (Archdeacon)—*continued.*

ESSAYS AND ADDRESSES. Crown 8vo.   2s. 6d. net.

GUARDIAN.—"We heartily welcome a new edition of Archdeacon Wilson's *Essays and Addresses.*"

SPEAKER.—"We are glad to welcome a new edition of the Archdeacon of Manchester's *Essays and Addresses.* . . . These addresses are manly, straightforward, and sagacious ; and they are, moreover, pervaded with a deep sense of responsibility and unfailing enthusiasm."

SOME CONTRIBUTIONS TO THE RELIGIOUS THOUGHT OF OUR TIME. Crown 8vo.   6s.

THE GOSPEL OF THE ATONEMENT.   Being the Hulsean Lectures for 1898. Crown 8vo.   3s. 6d.

SPEAKER.—"This volume deserves a cordial welcome, and will reward a careful study.   It is marked by a candour and courage, a sincerity and liberality of spirit, which prove very attractive."

OXFORD MAGAZINE.—"They contain a good deal of strong thought and delicate expression."

SPECTATOR.—"A notable pronouncement."

TWO SERMONS ON THE MUTUAL INFLUENCES OF THEOLOGY AND THE NATURAL SCIENCES. 8vo. Sewed.   6d. net.

LECTURES ON PASTORAL THEOLOGY.   Crown 8vo.
[*In the Press.*

Wood (C. J.)—SURVIVALS IN CHRISTIANITY. Cr. 8vo.   6s.

MANCHESTER GUARDIAN.—"Striking, stimulating and suggestive lectures. . . . The author writes with the boldness and conviction of a mystic ; he brings wide reading to bear upon every branch of his subject, and his book is impressive and interesting throughout."

Printed by R. & R. CLARK, LIMITED, *Edinburgh.*

5.3.03.

'7